I0530392

Goodbye, Friend: A Journey Through Pet Loss and Grieving

Emotional Healing and Comfort for Parents and Children Experiencing Grief from the Death of a Pet

Owen Whitmore

Copyright © 2024 by Owen Whitmore – All rights reserved.

The content within this book may not be reproduced, duplicated or transmitted without direct written permission from the author or the publisher.

Under no circumstances will any blame or legal responsibility be held against the publisher, or author, for any damages, reparation, or monetary loss due to the information contained within this book. Either directly or indirectly. You are responsible for your own choices, actions, and results.

Legal Notice:

This book is copyright protected. This book is only for personal use. You cannot amend, distribute, sell, use, quote or paraphrase any part, of the content within this book, without the consent of the author or publisher.

CONTENTS

INTRODUCTION

A few years ago, I sat on the steps of my home, my heart heavy with a profound ache that felt both familiar and foreign. My faithful companion, Max, a golden retriever with an insatiable love for tennis balls and muddy streams, had passed away at only eight years old from lymphoma. As I looked out at the empty yard, I remembered the countless afternoons we spent there. Max would chase after every throw, his joy as boundless as the horizon. His absence was palpable, leaving a void that seemed impossible to fill.

Losing a pet is a deeply personal journey, and yet, it is one that many of us share. The purpose of this book is to walk alongside you through this difficult time. It serves as a guide and companion, offering practical coping strategies and heartfelt ideas for memorializing your cherished friend. Together, we will navigate the depths of grief and work towards healing.

Pet ownership is a widespread phenomenon, with millions of households across the globe welcoming animals into their lives. Studies show that the bond between humans and pets is profound and enduring. When a pet passes away, the emotional impact is significant. This experience transcends age, culture, and background. It's a universal part of life, shared by many.

Your grief is real, and it is important. The loss of a beloved pet can feel overwhelming, akin to losing a family member or dear friend. It is crucial to recognize that your feelings are valid. You are not alone in this journey. Countless others have walked this path, and while each story is unique, the pain is a common thread that binds us.

This book is structured to aid you through each stage of your grieving process. In the initial chapters, we explore the nature of grief and how it manifests in the wake of pet loss. As we move forward, we delve into strategies to cope with the pain and begin the process of healing. Later sections focus on finding closure and exploring new beginnings. We also provide ideas for creating lasting memorials to honor the memory of your pet.

Amidst the sorrow, there is hope. Healing is a journey, one that takes time and patience. But it is possible to find comfort in the memories of your beloved pet. Remember the joy they brought into your life, the laughter, and the love. These memories are treasures that remain with you, even as you move forward.

As you read through this book, you will discover a wealth of coping mechanisms and healing practices. You'll find ways to memorialize your pet, creating a lasting tribute that honors their life and the joy they brought you. This book is designed to offer you support and guidance, ensuring you do not face this journey alone.

I invite you to turn the page and begin. Let us walk this path together, honoring the love and memories that remain.

CHAPTER 1

THE UNIQUE BOND: WHY PET LOSS HITS HARD

There's a poignant moment that sticks with me, an evening when my home felt remarkably quiet. The usual bustling sounds were absent—the gentle clinking of a collar, the soft padding of paws on the floor. After Max passed, it was the silence that struck me the hardest. Our pets weave themselves into the fabric of our daily lives so seamlessly that their absence is profoundly jarring. For those of us who have loved and lost a pet, the echoes of their presence linger long after they're gone. The loss of a pet feels intense and it's sometimes hard to understand the unique grief that follows.

Depth of the Human-Pet Relationship

The bond we share with our pets transcends the simple definition of animal companionship. They become our confidants, our comfort, and our constant source of joy. Every morning, they greet us with enthusiasm that never dims, whether it's our hundredth walk together or our thousandth shared breakfast. These daily rituals—the morning feeds, the evening cuddles, the weekend play sessions—create a tapestry of moments that define our relationships with our animal companions.

Consider how your pet fit into every aspect of your day. Perhaps they waited by the door when you returned from work, their excitement making even the most challenging day feel lighter. Maybe they curled up next to you during movie nights, their presence making solitude feel less lonely. These weren't just routines; they were the building blocks of a profound connection.

Pets see us at our most vulnerable. When tears fall, they press close, offering silent support. During illness, they maintain their vigil, their presence a constant comfort. Through divorce, job loss, or family struggles, they remain steadfast, never judging, always present. Their love doesn't waver based on our success or failure, our mood or circumstances. This unconditional acceptance creates a unique bond that can feel impossible to replace.

Research shows that interacting with pets lowers blood pressure, reduces stress hormones, and increases feel-good chemicals in our brains. But beyond these physiological benefits, our pets become emotional anchors. They help us maintain routine during chaotic times. They get us outside when depression tempts us to isolate. They make us laugh when we've forgotten how to smile.

Think about your own pet. Remember how they sensed your emotions, offering a paw or a purr just when you needed it most. Recall how their presence made your house feel like a home, their quirks and habits intertwined with your daily life. This deep integration into our lives explains why their loss creates such a profound void. It's not just the loss of a pet—it's the loss of a daily companion, a source of unconditional love, and a being who helped shape our routines and emotional well-being.

Pets are Non-Judgmental Companions

Unlike human relationships, which often come with expectations and judgment, our pets offer a rare form of pure acceptance. They don't care about our career choices, our relationship status, or our social standing. A pet's love remains constant whether we've received a promotion or lost our job, gained weight or lost it, succeeded or failed.

This absence of judgment creates a unique emotional safe haven. We can cry in front of our pets without feeling self-conscious. We can talk to them about our fears and insecurities without worrying about their response. They listen without offering unwanted advice or criticism. Their presence alone provides comfort, their silent support more powerful than words.

Consider moments of personal vulnerability. Perhaps you made a mistake at work, faced rejection, or struggled with self-doubt. While humans might offer well-meaning but sometimes hurtful feedback, your pet simply offered their presence. A dog's gentle head on your lap or a cat's soothing purr against your chest provided acceptance without conditions.

This emotional safety allows us to be fully ourselves. We don't need to maintain a facade or project strength when we feel weak. Our pets see us at our worst—in old pajamas, sick with the flu, or overwhelmed by life's challenges—and their affection never wavers. This consistent acceptance helps build our self-esteem and emotional resilience.

For many, pets become confidants during life's darkest moments. They witness our private struggles, our quiet tears, our moments of uncertainty. Their non-judgmental presence creates a space where we can process emotions honestly and openly. Whether dealing with anxiety, depression, or daily stress, pets offer silent support that helps us feel less alone.

This unconditional acceptance often makes the grief of losing a pet particularly acute. We're not just losing a companion; we're losing a being who provided emotional safety in a world that often feels judgmental and demanding. Understanding this unique aspect of the human-animal bond helps explain why the loss cuts so deep and why traditional platitudes about "just getting another pet" fall short of addressing our grief.

Impact of Losing a Daily Presence

The absence of a pet creates ripples through every corner of our daily lives. Empty food bowls gather dust in the kitchen. A leash hangs untouched by the door. The water dish sits dry, a stark reminder of what's missing. These physical traces of our pets become monuments to loss, turning ordinary household items into painful markers of their absence.

Each home holds different reminders. For dog owners, it might be the worn spot on the couch where their companion always perched to watch the world through the window. Cat owners might find themselves avoiding the sunny windowsill where their friend once stretched out for afternoon naps. The corner of a rug still bears the impression of a favorite sleeping spot. A scratching post stands unused. These silent witnesses to our shared life now echo with emptiness.

The disruption of daily routines cuts deeper than physical reminders. The morning alarm rings, but no eager face greets us. No paws tap across the floor, no familiar weight leans against our legs as we prepare breakfast. The simple act of making coffee becomes a reminder—no need to hurry through the morning walk, no food bowl to fill.

Our days lose their familiar rhythm. The after-work hours stretch longer without the welcome-home greeting. Evening walks disappear from our schedule. The nightly ritual of securing the house changes—no need to check the pet door, no final potty break before bed. Even sleep patterns shift without the familiar weight at our feet or the gentle sound of purring.

These disrupted routines leave us unanchored. Muscle memory betrays us—reaching to fill an empty bowl, calling out when returning home, moving carefully through dark rooms to avoid disturbing a pet who's no longer there. Each automatic action becomes a fresh reminder of loss.

The silence amplifies the absence. No clicking of nails on hardwood floors. No jingling collar tags. No subtle shifts and sighs in the night. This acoustic void can feel overwhelming, particularly during times our pets were most active—meal times, arrival times, play times. The house feels different, larger somehow, emptier than seems possible for the loss of such a small being.

Service Animals v. Companion Animals

The depth and nature of our bond with a pet significantly shapes our grieving journey. While all pet loss creates profound grief, the loss of a service animal introduces unique dimensions of mourning that extend beyond emotional attachment.

Service animals become extensions of their handler's independence and capability. Their loss creates a dual void—the absence of both a beloved companion and a vital support system. A guide dog's handler mourns not just their friend but also their trusted navigator, their bridge to confident mobility. The grief intertwines with practical challenges as daily tasks suddenly require new solutions.

The years of specialized training and partnership create intricate patterns of trust and cooperation. Service dogs learn to anticipate their handler's needs, developing an almost telepathic connection. This deep working bond adds layers to the grief process. Handlers often report feeling not just emotionally bereft but physically vulnerable, having lost both a companion and a crucial support system they relied on for daily functioning.

For those who worked with psychiatric service animals, the loss can trigger a cascade of mental health challenges. These animals provided vital emotional regulation, anxiety management, and crisis intervention. Their absence leaves a gap in established coping mechanisms, making the grieving process particularly complex as handlers navigate both emotional loss and the need to develop new support strategies.

Companion animal loss, while equally painful, follows different contours. These relationships, though profound, typically center on emotional connection rather than functional partnership. The grief focuses more on the loss of shared routines, affection, and the pure joy of companionship. The practical impact may be less severe, but the emotional void can feel just as vast.

Both types of bonds share common threads of grief—the empty space in our homes, the disrupted routines, the loss of unconditional love. However, service animal handlers often face additional challenges in processing their loss while simultaneously adapting to life without their assistance partner. This may require balancing emotional healing with practical considerations about future partnerships and training relationships.

Understanding these distinctions helps validate the unique aspects of each loss while recognizing that all pet grief deserves acknowledgment and support. Whether mourning a service partner or a beloved companion, the path through grief reflects the specific nature of the bond we shared.

Reflection

The journey through pet loss grief takes many forms, as unique as the bonds we share with our animal companions. Whether mourning a service animal or a family pet, the path forward begins with acknowledging the depth and validity of our grief.

The absence of judgment from our animal companions creates a special kind of safety—a space where we can be fully ourselves. This distinctive aspect of pet relationships often intensifies our grief, as we lose not just a companion but also that rare gift of complete acceptance.

Understanding these dynamics helps normalize the grief process. There's no timeline for healing, no prescribed way to navigate the empty spaces left behind. Each person's experience reflects their unique bond and circumstances.

For those who've lost service animals, the road may include additional challenges as they rebuild both emotional and practical aspects of their lives. Companion animal loss may focus more on emotional healing, but both experiences deserve equal validation and support.

Moving forward doesn't mean forgetting. Instead, it means learning to carry our memories with grace, allowing them to comfort rather than overwhelm. The routines we shared, the silent understanding, the countless small moments of connection—these become part of our story, shaping who we are and how we love.

Remember that grief is not a sign of weakness but a reflection of love's depth. Your feelings, whatever they may be, honor the relationship you shared with your pet. In the chapters ahead, we'll explore practical strategies for coping, ways to memorialize your companion, and paths toward healing while keeping their memory alive.

CHAPTER 2

EMOTIONAL ROLLERCOASTER: NAVIGATING INTENSE FEELINGS

Max, my beloved golden retriever, was the embodiment of unwavering loyalty and boundless affection. His soulful eyes held a depth that transcended mere companionship, offering solace during life's emotional rollercoasters. In the depths of despair, his gentle presence provided a safe harbor, a reminder that love could weather any storm. Conversely, in moments of joy, his infectious enthusiasm amplified the euphoria, his wagging tail a metronome of pure delight. Navigating the emotional terrain alongside Max was a dance of give-and-take, his steadfast spirit grounding me when the world seemed unsteady, and his playful antics lifting me to soar when life's burdens felt too heavy.

Identifying Ranges of Emotions

The journey through pet loss grief twists and turns through a landscape of complex emotions. Each feeling serves as a natural response to the profound connection we shared with our animal companions. Let's explore these emotions to help you understand and process your experience.

Sadness manifests in different ways. You might find yourself breaking down at the sight of an empty food bowl or bursting into tears when passing your pet's favorite park. This depth of sorrow reflects the magnitude of your love and the space your pet occupied in your daily life.

Anger often catches grieving pet owners by surprise. You might feel rage at the veterinarian who couldn't save your companion, or at the illness that took them too soon. Some direct their anger inward, questioning if they could have done more or noticed symptoms earlier. These feelings, while difficult, represent a normal part of the grieving process.

The decision to euthanize brings its own unique burden of guilt. Questions like "Did I act too soon?" or "Should I have waited longer?" can haunt even the most rational mind. This guilt stems from the immense responsibility of making end-of-life decisions for our beloved pets. Remember that choosing to end suffering comes from a place of deep love and compassion.

For those who cared for chronically ill pets, relief often mingles with sorrow after their passing. This relief doesn't diminish your love - it acknowledges the weight of caretaking and the peace that comes from knowing your pet no longer suffers. Yet this feeling frequently triggers another wave of guilt, creating a complex emotional cycle that needs gentle understanding and acceptance.

Each emotion deserves acknowledgment and respect. There's no "right" way to feel when grieving a pet. Some experience these emotions in waves, while others find certain feelings more prominent than others. The key lies in recognizing these responses as valid expressions of your loss.

Emotions that Accompany Pet Loss

Grief rarely follows a predictable path. One moment you might feel acceptance, only to find yourself overwhelmed with sadness the next. These emotional swings represent a natural response to loss, not a sign of weakness or instability.

Unexpected triggers can spark powerful reactions. The jingle of keys might remind you of how your dog used to race to the door. A sunny windowsill might evoke memories of your cat's favorite napping spot. These moments can bring sudden tears, even weeks or months after your loss. Such reactions might feel embarrassing, especially in public places or around people who don't understand the depth of pet loss grief. Know that these emotional responses reflect the genuine bond you shared with your pet.

Yet amid the tears, you might find yourself smiling at cherished memories. The way your cat would sprint through the house at 3 AM, creating a thunderous symphony of paws against hardwood floors. Or how your dog's tail wagged so hard during dinner prep that his whole body shook, eyes locked on every move you made in the kitchen. These moments of joy don't diminish your grief - they honor the happiness your pet brought to your life.

Some people feel guilty about experiencing happiness after their pet's death. They might think laughing or enjoying life somehow betrays their pet's memory. But finding moments of joy amidst grief shows the lasting positive impact your pet had on your life. Your pet brought you happiness in life; their memory can continue to bring comfort and even laughter.

The unpredictable nature of grief might leave you feeling unsteady. One day you might handle looking at photos of your pet with calm reflection, while the next day the sight of their favorite toy reduces you to tears. This emotional rollercoaster represents the process of adjusting to life without your companion's physical presence.

Remember that no timeline exists for "proper" grieving. Some days will feel lighter than others. You might experience weeks of relative calm followed by intense waves of emotion triggered by anniversaries, holidays, or random memories. Each person's journey through pet loss differs, shaped by their unique relationship with their animal companion and their individual way of processing loss.

Managing Emotional Swings

Managing the emotional waves of pet loss requires gentle, practical approaches that honor both your grief and your need to function in daily life. Let's explore some strategies that can help you navigate these challenging moments.

Breathing exercises offer immediate relief when emotions threaten to overwhelm. Try this simple technique: Inhale slowly through your nose for a count of four, hold for four, then exhale through your mouth for a count of six. This pattern signals your nervous system to calm down, providing a moment of peace when grief feels too heavy. Practice this exercise anywhere - at your desk, in your car, or when passing your pet's favorite spots around the house.

Creating a grief journal provides a private space to express your deepest feelings without judgment. Don't worry about grammar or structure - simply let your thoughts flow onto the page. Record moments when grief hits hardest, but also document times when memories bring comfort or even joy. This practice helps track your emotional patterns and identify specific triggers.

Consider these journaling prompts:

- What moments with my pet brought the most happiness today?

- When did I feel overwhelmed by their absence?

- What physical sensations accompany my grief?

- Which coping strategies helped most today?

Your journal might reveal that mornings feel particularly difficult, or that certain locations trigger intense emotions. This awareness helps you prepare for challenging moments and adjust your daily routine accordingly. Some people find comfort in maintaining two columns: one for recording difficult moments, another for noting instances of peace or acceptance.

Remember to date your entries. Looking back over time often reveals subtle shifts in your grief journey, showing progress that might otherwise go unnoticed. Some days might fill several pages, while others warrant just a few words. Both are equally valid expressions of your experience.

Combined with breathing exercises, journaling creates a powerful toolkit for emotional regulation. When you feel waves of grief building, pause for a few deep breaths, then reach for your journal. This two-step approach helps process intense emotions while creating a meaningful record of your journey through loss.

Emotional Resilience

Building emotional resilience during pet loss requires a combination of self-care practices and professional support. While grief can feel isolating, reaching out for help demonstrates strength, not weakness. Professional counseling specifically focused on pet loss has grown more accessible and accepted in recent years.

A grief counselor provides valuable tools for processing complex emotions. They create a safe space to express feelings without judgment, especially helpful when friends or family minimize pet loss grief. These professionals understand the unique challenges of pet bereavement and can offer specialized coping strategies.

Look for counselors who:

- Specialize in pet loss or grief counseling

- Offer both individual and group therapy options

- Provide flexible scheduling for crisis moments

- Demonstrate understanding of the human-animal bond

Creative expression offers another powerful avenue for processing grief. Art, music, writing, or crafting can help release emotions that feel too complex for words. These activities engage different parts of the brain, allowing grief to flow through alternative channels.

Consider these creative approaches:

- Paint or draw your pet's portrait

- Create a memory box with photos and mementos

- Write poetry about your experiences together

- Compose music inspired by your pet's personality

- Craft a memorial garden or plant a remembrance tree

The act of creation itself can provide moments of peace. Working with your hands occupies the conscious mind while allowing deeper emotions to surface naturally. Many find that creative projects help maintain a connection with their pet while processing their loss.

Don't worry about artistic skill levels. The therapeutic value lies in the process, not the final product. Some find that abstract art better expresses their emotional state than realistic representations. Others prefer functional projects like quilting with their pet's old blankets or creating scrapbooks of shared memories.

These creative outlets can also serve as conversation starters, helping you share your grief journey with others who understand. Consider joining pet loss support groups where members often share their memorial projects and creative expressions of grief.

Reflection

The journey through pet loss transforms us. While the pain may soften over time, our pets leave permanent imprints on our hearts. Building emotional resilience doesn't mean forgetting - it means learning to carry our memories with grace while remaining open to love again.

Remember that healing isn't linear. Some days will feel lighter, while others may bring unexpected waves of grief. This unpredictability is normal and doesn't reflect backwards progress. Each emotional surge helps process the loss more deeply.

Practice self-compassion during difficult moments. Treat yourself with the same kindness your pet always showed you. Take breaks when needed, rest when overwhelmed, and celebrate small victories in your grief journey.

Your capacity for resilience grows stronger through:

- Maintaining routines and self-care practices

- Connecting with others who understand pet loss

- Honoring your pet's memory through meaningful activities

- Allowing yourself to experience joy without guilt

- Seeking support when grief feels overwhelming

The tools and strategies shared here serve as stepping stones toward healing. Your grief journey is uniquely yours, but you don't have to walk it alone. Whether through counseling, creative expression, or community support, resources exist to help you navigate this challenging time.

Take what resonates from these pages and leave what doesn't serve you. Trust your instincts about what feels right for your healing process. Most importantly, be patient with yourself as you learn to carry both your love and your loss.

The bond you shared with your pet remains unbroken, even as you grow stronger through grief. Let their memory inspire you to move forward with an open heart, knowing that building resilience honors the love they brought to your life.

CHAPTER 3

THE STAGES OF GRIEF: APPLYING THEM TO PET LOSS

T hose first few days after Max passed felt like an endless fog. The house seemed unnaturally quiet without his playful barks greeting me or his nails clicking across the hardwood floors. I caught myself instinctively reaching for his leash when heading out, only to be reminded he was gone. Denial gave way to profound sadness as I struggled to accept the reality of his absence. Anger soon followed - I railed against the cruel injustice of his life being cut short by illness. Mundane tasks like washing his bowls or packing away his toys unleashed fresh waves of anguish. But slowly, precious memories began resurfacing through the grief, sparking bittersweet smiles amidst the tears.

When we experience the loss of a beloved pet, we often find ourselves navigating through a spectrum of emotions that can feel as unpredictable as they are overwhelming. The stages of grief, a model first introduced by Dr. Elisabeth Kübler-Ross, provide a framework to understand these emotions. Traditionally, these stages include denial, anger, bargaining, depression, and acceptance. While these stages were initially conceived to explain human loss, they are equally relevant to the grief experienced after losing a pet. Each stage offers insight into the emotional landscape that many of us traverse during this difficult time.

Stage 1: Denial

The house felt eerily quiet without Max's familiar panting and the click of his nails on the hardwood floor. I wandered aimlessly, half-expecting to see his tail wagging around every corner. Clutching his worn leash, I fought the urge to call out his name, knowing he wouldn't come bounding towards me anymore.

"He's just out in the yard," I told myself, glancing at the front door. Any minute now, that jingling collar would announce his return. But as the minutes ticked by, reality began to sink in – a harsh truth I desperately wanted to deny.

The first stage, denial, often emerges in the moments after learning of a pet's terminal diagnosis or death. Denial serves as the mind's natural defense mechanism, a buffer against the immediate shock of loss. For many, this manifests in subtle ways - catching glimpses of their pet in familiar spots around the house, hearing phantom scratches at the door, or maintaining daily routines as if their companion were still present.

This protective numbness can last hours, days, or even weeks. Some pet owners find themselves making future plans that include their deceased pet - booking veterinary appointments or buying their favorite treats - only to face the painful reminder of reality moments later.

Medical professionals and grief counselors recognize denial as a crucial part of the grieving process. It allows our minds to process loss at a manageable pace, preventing us from becoming overwhelmed by the full weight of our emotions all at once.

For others, denial manifests as a refusal to remove their pet's belongings or disturb their favorite spots. A dog's water bowl remains filled, a cat's perch untouched, their toys left exactly where they last played with them. These actions, while appearing irrational to others, represent a natural response to profound loss.

This stage of grief doesn't follow a predetermined timeline. Some may move through it quickly, while others might find themselves cycling back to moments of denial even after accepting their loss. Understanding that this response is normal and natural can help pet owners navigate this challenging phase of their grief journey.

Stage 2: Anger

In the weeks after Max's passing, anger simmered beneath my sorrow like molten rock. Irrational resentment bubbled up over mundane annoyances—a dropped dish or traffic delay unleashing my rage. Bitter thoughts consumed me as I replayed his final moments, furious at the unfairness of his life cut short. Regrets tormented me endlessly. If only I'd taken him to the vet sooner...if only I'd been more attentive...if only... The anger scorched my soul, manifesting as harsh snapping at loved ones trying to console me. I felt cruel, adrift in turbulent emotional waters with no anchor. Unmoored by loss, I drifted dangerously close to the dark rocks of self-destruction before finally letting the waves of grief carry me back to calmer shores.

As denial begins to fade, anger can surface. This raw, intense emotion often catches pet owners off guard with its ferocity. This anger might not have a clear target—it can be directed at circumstances, others, or even oneself. The frustration of losing a pet can feel unjust, and it's common to lash out in a search for blame. You might find yourself angry at the world for taking away your cherished companion, or at yourself for not doing more.

Pet owners might find themselves lashing out at well-meaning friends who say things like "it was just a dog" or "you can always get another cat." These dismissive comments, though often unintentional, can ignite a fierce protective rage. The anger stems from a deep place of love and loss, a testament to the profound bond shared with our animal companions.

For those whose pets died due to accidents or negligence, anger may focus on specific individuals or circumstances. A neighbor who left a gate open, a driver who wasn't paying attention, or a manufacturer whose product proved harmful - these become targets for the pain that needs somewhere to go.

Sometimes, anger turns inward. Pet owners torture themselves with "what-ifs" and "if-onlys." Could they have noticed the symptoms sooner?

Should they have sought a second opinion? Would a different food or treatment have made a difference? These questions fuel a cycle of self-directed rage that can be particularly difficult to break.

The intensity of anger following pet loss often surprises people who haven't experienced it. Society tends to minimize pet grief, which can make pet owners feel isolated in their anger or ashamed of its intensity. Yet anger represents a natural and necessary part of the grieving process, one that deserves acknowledgment and respect.

Stage 3: Bargaining

I pored over his medical records, searching for some missed detail or alternative treatment we'd overlooked. Maybe if we'd tried that experimental drug or sought a second opinion from another specialist...

"I'll do anything," I whispered feverishly, as if striking a deal with the universe. A piece of my soul still clung to the impossible hope of regaining more time with him. If only I could go back and make different choices, perhaps the outcome would change.

The bargaining stage of pet grief often intertwines with hope and desperation, manifesting in countless "if only" scenarios. Pet owners replay moments leading up to their loss, searching for points where different choices might have changed the outcome. These mental negotiations can consume hours, days, or weeks of thought.

"If I had noticed the symptoms sooner..." becomes a haunting refrain. Pet owners dissect every interaction, every subtle change in behavior they might have missed. They bargain with the past, promising impossible things in exchange for more time - better care, more attention, or lifestyle changes they believe might have prevented their loss.

This bargaining extends beyond rational thought. Some pet owners find themselves making deals with higher powers, promising dramatic life changes in exchange for their pet's return or recovery. A woman might pledge to volunteer at shelters for the rest of her life if her cat survives surgery. A man might swear to never miss a morning walk again if his dog pulls through one more night.

For those facing end-of-life decisions, bargaining takes on additional complexity. They negotiate with veterinarians, seeking alternative treatments or experimental procedures. Financial considerations that once seemed important fade away as they offer to pay any price, take any loan, or make any sacrifice to save their companion.

Even after loss, bargaining continues. Pet owners bargain with their memories, trying to preserve every detail of their time together. They negotiate with their grief, making deals about when they'll allow themselves to cry or when they'll try to move forward. Some bargain with themselves about getting another pet, setting conditions and timelines that feel like betrayal one moment and healing the next.

The bargaining stage reveals the depth of love and attachment we form with our pets. These mental negotiations, though ultimately futile, serve as a natural part of processing loss. They represent our mind's attempt to regain control in a situation where we feel powerless, to find order in the chaos of grief.

Stage 4: Depression

The house remained still and lifeless without Max's joyful energy filling every corner. I drifted through the motions of each day, his absence a constant, crushing weight.

Sunlight filtered through the windows, but the warmth never quite reached me. I curled up on the couch he used to nap beside me, letting the emptiness swallow me whole as I surrendered to the depths of sorrow.

Depression during pet loss manifests in unique ways that can catch even the most resilient person off guard. The empty food bowl in the kitchen might trigger waves of sadness. The unused leash hanging by the door becomes a painful reminder. Even the simplest daily tasks—like coming home to a quiet house or eating dinner without a hopeful face watching from beneath the table—can feel overwhelming.

This stage often brings physical symptoms alongside emotional ones. Sleep patterns may change dramatically. Some find themselves sleeping more than usual, seeking escape in slumber, while others lie awake, their minds replaying memories of their pet. Appetite changes are common too—food might lose its appeal, or comfort eating might become a temporary coping mechanism.

Social withdrawal is another hallmark of this stage. The world continues to turn while you're frozen in grief, and this disconnect can feel isolating. Well-meaning friends might struggle to understand the depth of your loss, offering platitudes like "it was just a pet" or "you can always get another one." These comments, though often intended to help, can deepen the sense of loneliness and misunderstanding.

The depression stage also brings unexpected triggers. A commercial featuring a similar breed of dog, the sound of a cat purring on TV, or even passing your pet's favorite park can unleash fresh waves of grief. These moments might feel like setbacks, but they're natural parts of processing loss.

During this stage, many people may still question their decision-making around their pet's final days. Did they wait too long to say goodbye? Should they have tried different treatments? This self-doubt can compound the depression, creating a cycle of grief and guilt that feels impossible to break.

The physical space once occupied by your pet becomes charged with emotion. The corner where their bed used to be, the window perch they claimed as their own, or the specific spot on the couch where they always curled up—these places become monuments to absence. Some find themselves avoiding these spaces entirely, while others find comfort in maintaining them exactly as they were.

It's important to understand that these stages are not linear. You might find yourself revisiting anger on the anniversary of your pet's passing or feeling acceptance alongside moments of deep sadness.

Stage 5: Acceptance

The first few months without Max felt like an endless fog of emptiness. His absence left a cavernous void in the daily routines we had grown so accustomed to over the years. The house seemed eerily quiet without his familiar panting or the rhythmic thump of his wagging tail. Slowly, memories of Max began emerging from the haze of grief. The joyful recollections of his boundless energy and unconditional affection helped shift the heaviness. While I would never stop missing him, acceptance bloomed - he lived a full, love-filled life, and I felt grateful for the time we shared.

Acceptance arrives not as a sudden revelation but as gentle shifts in perspective. The morning you wake up and can smile at a photo of your pet without crying. The moment you share a funny story about them without your voice breaking. These small victories mark the gradual transition toward a new normal.

This stage doesn't mean forgetting or "getting over" the loss of your pet. Instead, acceptance transforms raw grief into tender remembrance. You might find yourself able to pack away their belongings while keeping a few special items displayed. Their collar becomes a treasured keepsake rather than a source of pain. Their favorite toy moves from the floor to a shelf, now a cherished memorial rather than a reminder of absence.

During acceptance, many people discover ways to honor their pet's memory that bring comfort rather than sorrow. Creating a photo album, planting a memorial garden, or volunteering at an animal shelter helps channel grief into meaningful action. These activities acknowledge the continuing bond with your pet while allowing space for healing.

The acceptance stage also brings a deeper understanding of the impact your pet had on your life. You begin to recognize how they shaped your routines, relationships, and even your character. Their influence remains, woven into the fabric of your daily existence. The walks you took together might have made you more observant of nature. Their unconditional love might have taught you patience or compassion.

Physical spaces that once felt haunted by absence slowly transform. The empty corner where their bed sat might become a reading nook decorated with their photo. The backyard where they played becomes a garden dedicated to their memory. These changes don't erase their presence but integrate it into your new reality.

During acceptance, you might find yourself open to new possibilities while still honoring your lost companion. The thought of loving another pet no longer feels like betrayal. You understand that each relationship is unique, and opening your heart again doesn't diminish the special bond you shared.

The Non-Linear Journey of Pet Loss Grief

Grief doesn't follow a neat roadmap. While understanding the stages helps provide context for our emotions, the reality of pet loss grief often feels more like a maze than a straight path. You might experience acceptance one day, only to find yourself plunged back into denial or anger the next.

These emotional shifts don't indicate regression or failure in your healing journey. They're natural responses to triggers that remind you of your pet. The first snowfall might bring back memories of their excitement, causing a fresh wave of sadness. Their birthday or adoption anniversary might reignite feelings of anger about their loss. Even years later, finding an old photo or toy can temporarily transport you back to earlier stages of grief.

Certain milestones often spark intense emotional responses. The first holiday season without your pet, the anniversary of their passing, or even routine events like vet appointments for other pets can resurface complex feelings. You might find yourself bargaining again - "If only I had noticed the symptoms sooner" - even after months of acceptance.

Depression can coexist with acceptance in surprising ways. You might feel at peace with your pet's passing while still experiencing profound sadness about their absence. This duality is perfectly normal. Some days you'll celebrate the joy they brought to your life, while others you'll mourn the future moments you won't share.

The key is recognizing that this back-and-forth movement between grief stages reflects the depth of your bond rather than any failure to "move on." Each return to a previous stage often brings new insights and understanding. The anger you feel six months after loss might focus more on missing their presence rather than the circumstances of their death. The denial that surfaces years later might manifest as brief moments of expecting to see them in their favorite spots rather than disbelief about their passing.

This non-linear journey requires patience and self-compassion. Some days will feel like steps backward, but they're actually opportunities for deeper healing and integration of your loss experience.

Reflection

The journey through pet loss grief follows no predetermined path. Each person's experience is as unique as the bond they shared with their companion animal. Understanding these stages of grief—denial, anger, bargaining, depression, and acceptance—provides a framework for processing loss, but it's essential to remember that grief rarely follows a linear progression.

These stages serve as guideposts rather than rigid checkpoints. You might skip certain stages entirely or cycle through them multiple times. Some days might bring unexpected waves of sadness long after you've reached acceptance, while others might offer surprising moments of peace during the depths of grief. This fluctuation is normal and natural.

The key lies not in rushing through these stages but in allowing yourself to experience each emotion fully and authentically. Just as your relationship with your pet was unique, your grief journey will be distinctly your own. There's no "right" way to grieve, no prescribed timeline for healing, and no shame in seeking support when needed.

Remember that acknowledging and understanding these stages of grief doesn't diminish the depth of your loss. Instead, it provides a framework for processing your emotions and validates the profound impact our animal companions have on our lives. Your grief is a testament to the love you shared, and working through it honors the memory of your beloved pet.

As we move forward, we'll explore practical strategies for coping with each stage of grief, methods for memorializing your pet, and ways to find support within the pet loss community. Your journey of healing has already begun, and understanding these stages represents an important first step toward finding peace while keeping your pet's memory alive in your heart.

CHAPTER 4

COMMON MISCONCEPTIONS: DEBUNKING MYTHS ABOUT PET GRIEF

I n the dimly lit bedroom, I sat cross-legged on the floor, clutching Max's worn-out tennis ball—the one he loved chasing until his final days. The indentations from his teeth served as a poignant reminder of our endless games of fetch. Tears streamed down my face as I grappled with the profound emptiness left by his absence.

One of the cruelest myths surrounding pet grief is the notion that it's somehow less significant than the loss of a human loved one. But for those of us who have opened our hearts and homes to these remarkable creatures, their passing leaves a cavernous void. Max wasn't just a pet; he was a loyal companion, a source of unconditional love, and an integral part of my daily life for over a decade.

Another harmful misconception is that grief should follow a linear progression, neatly compartmentalized into distinct stages. In reality, the emotions associated with pet loss ebb and flow like ocean tides, sometimes crashing unexpectedly and other times retreating to a gentle swell. There were moments when I found solace in acceptance, only to be blindsided by overwhelming sadness triggered by the smallest reminder—a squeaky toy under the couch or the jingling of his collar.

Validating Your Grief

Society often fails to recognize the profound impact of losing a pet. While the death of a human family member brings casseroles, sympathy cards, and time off work, the loss of an animal companion frequently goes unacknowledged. Well-meaning friends might suggest "getting another pet" or remind you that "it was just a dog." These dismissive responses can deepen your pain and isolate you in your grief.

The truth is, pet loss grief is real, valid, and deserves recognition. Research has consistently shown that the human-animal bond creates genuine emotional attachments comparable to human relationships. The unconditional love, daily companionship, and physical affection shared with pets forge neural pathways in our brains similar to those formed in parent-child relationships.

When someone says, "It's just an animal," they reveal their own lack of understanding rather than any truth about your loss. Modern science has demolished this outdated perspective. Studies demonstrate that pets reduce stress hormones, lower blood pressure, and improve mental health. The death of a pet disrupts these biological and emotional connections, triggering genuine grief responses in our bodies and minds.

The misunderstanding of the human-animal bond stems from outdated cultural attitudes that view animals as property rather than family members. Yet anyone who has shared their life with a pet knows the depth of these relationships. Your pet witnessed your daily struggles, celebrated your victories, and provided unwavering support through life's challenges. They were present for countless intimate moments, from midnight anxiety attacks to morning coffee rituals.

This bond isn't diminished by species differences - it's often enhanced by them. Unlike human relationships complicated by judgment, expectations, and conflicting needs, the pure simplicity of pet love creates unique emotional safety.

Your pet never criticized your choices, held grudges, or withheld affection. This unconditional acceptance creates a profound connection that deserves to be honored in its loss.

Your grief is legitimate. The emptiness you feel is real. Don't let anyone minimize your loss or rush your healing process. Understanding and accepting the validity of your grief marks an essential step toward processing it in healthy ways.

Taking Time to Grieve

In our fast-paced world, there's intense pressure to "get over" losses quickly and return to normal functioning. This expectation becomes especially challenging with pet loss, where others might assume you should bounce back within days or weeks. The common refrain "When are you getting another pet?" often comes before you've even processed your grief.

There is no universal timeline for pet loss grief. Some people may feel ready to welcome a new pet after a few months, while others need years before considering that possibility. Both responses are valid. Your grief journey belongs to you alone, and attempting to conform to arbitrary timelines can hinder genuine healing.

Cultural expectations around pet loss vary widely. Some societies honor animal companions with formal rituals and designated mourning periods, while others dismiss such grief entirely. In the United States, the lack of established mourning customs for pets often leaves bereaved pet owners without clear guidance or support systems.

The pressure to "move on" quickly can manifest in various ways:

These external pressures often conflict with your internal healing process. Grief doesn't operate on a schedule. It ebbs and flows, sometimes intensifying months after the loss when others expect you to have "gotten over it."

Research shows that suppressing grief to meet others' expectations can lead to complicated mourning and delayed healing. Instead of forcing yourself to adhere to artificial timelines, focus on honoring your authentic emotional experience. This might mean:

Remember that grief isn't measured in days or weeks - it's measured in healing moments and personal growth. Your timeline is yours alone.

Acknowledging Your Grief

Pet loss grief deserves recognition and respect. Studies have shown that the death of a beloved animal companion can trigger the same neurological and emotional responses as losing a human family member. Your brain doesn't distinguish between species when processing loss - it responds to the severing of a meaningful bond.

Suppressing or minimizing your grief can lead to serious mental health consequences. When society fails to validate your loss, you might question the legitimacy of your emotions or feel shame for "overreacting." This invalidation often results in:

Research from the Human-Animal Bond Research Institute reveals that 90% of pet owners consider their animals family members. This deep connection means the loss creates a genuine void in your life. Your pet likely played multiple roles - companion, confidant, source of routine, and emotional support. Their absence affects every aspect of daily living.

Acknowledging your grief means giving yourself permission to:

Mental health professionals increasingly recognize pet loss as a significant life event requiring support and intervention. Many now offer specialized counseling for animal companion loss, understanding that unprocessed grief can evolve into complicated mourning patterns.

Your grief is real. Your pain matters. The depth of your sorrow reflects the depth of your love, and there's nothing wrong or shameful about mourning the loss of a being who brought such joy and meaning to your life. By acknowledging your grief, you take the first step toward authentic healing.

Common Misconceptions About Pet Loss Grief

One of the most damaging myths surrounding pet loss is the notion that you should "get over it" by immediately adopting another animal. Well-meaning friends might suggest visiting the local shelter just days after your loss, believing that a new pet will ease your pain. This misguided advice overlooks the crucial need for processing grief and can lead to complicated emotional responses.

Every animal has a unique personality, relationship dynamic, and place in your heart. Attempting to "replace" your deceased pet dismisses the singular bond you shared and may create unfair expectations for a new companion. Your grief deserves space and time to unfold naturally.

Another prevalent misconception centers around the need for formal closure. Some believe that without a traditional funeral or burial service, proper grieving cannot occur. While ceremonies and rituals can provide comfort, they aren't mandatory for healing. Your grieving process belongs to you alone.

Many pet owners feel pressured to maintain a stoic facade, especially when others minimize their loss. Society often expects people to "move on" quickly after pet loss, suggesting that prolonged grief indicates emotional weakness. This stigma can prevent individuals from seeking necessary support or expressing their feelings openly.

The truth is that grief follows no predetermined timeline or format. Some find solace in creating memory boxes or photo albums. Others prefer private moments of remembrance. There's no "correct" way to honor your pet's memory or process your loss.

Common grieving myths to reject:

Your journey through pet loss is personal and valid. Trust your instincts about what feels right for your healing process, regardless of others' expectations or assumptions.

Reflection

The journey through pet loss grief challenges many societal assumptions and misconceptions. Understanding these common myths helps validate your emotional experience and creates space for authentic healing. By recognizing that your grief is legitimate, personal, and deserving of respect, you can begin processing your loss in ways that feel genuine to you.

Society's expectations about pet loss often conflict with the reality of the deep bonds we forge with our animal companions. These relationships, built on unconditional love and daily intimacy, create profound emotional connections that deserve proper acknowledgment when broken. Your grief isn't measured by others' standards or timelines - it's shaped by your unique experience and relationship with your pet.

The pressure to "bounce back" quickly or hide your feelings can compound the pain of loss. Remember that taking time to grieve, seeking support, and honoring your pet's memory are healthy responses to loss. Whether you choose to memorialize your pet through ceremonies, artwork, or quiet reflection, your chosen path is valid.

Moving forward doesn't mean forgetting. Your pet's impact on your life remains significant, and carrying those memories honors the relationship you shared. Give yourself permission to grieve openly, honestly, and for as long as necessary. Your healing journey belongs to you alone.

By understanding and rejecting these misconceptions, you create space for authentic grieving and genuine healing. Trust your instincts, honor your emotions, and remember that your pet's love enriched your life in ways that deserve to be acknowledged and celebrated.

CHAPTER 5

THE "WHAT IFS" AND "SHOULD HAVES": RELEASING REGRETS

The memories of Max still linger, both joyful and bittersweet. His wagging tail and soulful eyes greet me each time I reminisce about our years together. Yet, the "what ifs" and "should haves" creep in, casting shadows over those cherished moments.

What if I had taken him to the vet sooner when he first showed signs of discomfort? Maybe they could have caught his illness earlier and prolonged his quality of life. Or perhaps I should have been more diligent about his diet, ensuring he received the proper nutrients to support his aging body.

The nagging voice in my head wonders if I could have done more to ease his suffering towards the end. Should I have explored alternative therapies or sought a second opinion? Did I make the right decision when the time came to let him go?

These thoughts swirl endlessly, each one a pang of guilt and self-doubt. But then I remember Max's unwavering love and loyalty, his ability to live in the present moment without regrets or worries about the future.

Breaking Free from the "What If" Cycle

The human mind gravitates toward replaying difficult moments, searching for alternate paths and different outcomes. After losing a pet, these thoughts can become particularly intense and persistent. Pet owners often find themselves trapped in an endless loop of "what if" scenarios, questioning every decision made during their pet's life, especially near the end.

"If only I had noticed the symptoms sooner."

"What if I had chosen a different treatment?"

"Should I have waited longer before making that final decision?"

These thoughts represent a natural part of the grieving process, yet they can become overwhelming. The tendency to second-guess past decisions stems from our deep love for our pets and our desire to have done everything possible for them. We replay conversations with veterinarians, scrutinize treatment choices, and question timing - all in an attempt to find certainty in situations that offered none.

The weight of medical decisions, particularly those made during emergency situations or end-of-life care, can feel especially heavy. Pet owners often struggle with choices made under pressure, wondering if different decisions might have led to better outcomes. The responsibility of being our pets' voice in medical matters can leave us vulnerable to doubt and self-questioning long after they're gone.

Even routine care decisions can become sources of retrospective anxiety. We might question past diet choices, exercise routines, or preventive care measures. The mind can fixate on seemingly minor details - a delayed vet visit, a missed medication dose, or an extra treat given despite health restrictions.

These thoughts tend to surface most strongly during quiet moments: late at night when sleep proves elusive, during daily activities that remind us of our pet, or on significant dates like anniversaries. The "what if" cycle can feel like a maze with no exit, each question leading to another, each scenario branching into countless possibilities.

This pattern of thinking reflects our struggle to accept circumstances beyond our control. It's a manifestation of our wish to have changed the outcome, to have found a way to keep our beloved pets with us longer.

Hindsight Bias

Looking back at past decisions with the knowledge we have today creates a deceptive lens. When grieving a pet, this distortion becomes particularly painful as we judge our past choices through the clarity of hindsight. This perspective trick of the mind - known as hindsight bias - can transform reasonable decisions made with limited information into sources of guilt and regret.

Consider the common scenario of a pet showing subtle changes in behavior. At the time, these might have seemed like normal variations - a day of decreased appetite, slight lethargy, or minor changes in routine. Without the benefit of knowing what would develop later, these signs might not have raised immediate alarm. Yet after a serious diagnosis or loss, these same moments can feel like glaring red flags we "should have" recognized.

The reality is that we make decisions based on the information available to us in the moment. A pet owner who delays a vet visit for what appears to be a minor issue is not being negligent - they're making a reasonable judgment based on their experience and current understanding. The fact that this decision looks different in retrospect doesn't change the validity of the choice when it was made.

Medical decisions, in particular, suffer from this distortion. The path that seems obvious after knowing the outcome was rarely clear in the moment. Veterinary medicine often involves weighing multiple factors, considering quality of life, and making choices without perfect information. A treatment plan that proved unsuccessful wasn't necessarily wrong - it may have been the best option given the circumstances and available knowledge at the time.

This bias can manifest in seemingly endless ways:

- "The symptoms were so obvious now that I think about it."

- "I should have known something was wrong."

- "Why didn't I get a second opinion sooner?"

- "If only I had researched more thoroughly."

These thoughts ignore the reality that we cannot make decisions with information we don't yet have. Understanding hindsight bias doesn't eliminate the pain of loss, but it can help us be kinder to ourselves about the choices we made while caring for our pets.

Letting Go of Regrets

While understanding hindsight bias helps explain our thought patterns, actively working to release these regrets requires dedicated practice and self-compassion. One powerful technique involves writing letters to yourself, addressing the specific decisions that weigh heavily on your mind.

Find a quiet space and take out paper and pen. Begin your letter with "Dear [Your Name]," and write from a place of understanding rather than judgment. Acknowledge the circumstances you faced at the time, the information you had available, and the love that motivated your choices. Express forgiveness for any perceived mistakes or oversights, remembering that you made the best decisions possible with the knowledge you had.

These letters serve as tangible reminders of your journey and can be revisited whenever guilt resurfaces. Some pet owners find it helpful to ceremonially release these letters - perhaps by burning them safely or burying them in a meaningful location - as a symbolic act of letting go.

Practicing gratitude offers another path toward healing. Instead of focusing on what you wish you had done differently, redirect your energy toward appreciation for the time you shared with your pet. Create a gratitude journal dedicated to memories of your companion. Each day, write down one specific moment you're thankful for:

- The way they greeted you after work

- Their unique quirks and personalities

- The comfort they provided during difficult times

- The lessons they taught you about love and patience

- The simple joy of their presence in your daily routine

This shift from regret to gratitude doesn't deny the pain of loss or invalidate your feelings. Rather, it helps balance the difficult emotions with recognition of the gift it was to share your life with your pet. Every moment of joy, every act of care, every decision made from love - these all matter more than the what-ifs that haunt us.

Remember that letting go of regret is a gradual process. Some days will feel easier than others, and that's okay. The goal isn't to eliminate these thoughts entirely but to develop a gentler relationship with them when they arise.

Reframing Our Thoughts

The way we think about our loss shapes our healing journey. When grief overwhelms us, our minds often fixate on the difficult final moments - the last visit to the vet, the moment of goodbye, or the empty food bowl we couldn't bring ourselves to put away. These thoughts, while natural, can prevent us from accessing the full spectrum of memories we share with our beloved pets.

Reframing involves consciously redirecting our focus toward the positive aspects of our pet's life and our shared experiences. Instead of dwelling on their final day, recall their first day home. Remember the excitement in their eyes, the way they explored their new environment, or how they chose their favorite spot in the house.

When memories of illness surface, balance them with recollections of health and vitality. Think about:

- The enthusiasm they showed during walks or playtime

- Their favorite games and toys

- Special holiday moments you shared

- Quiet evenings spent together

- The unique ways they showed their love

Create a memory book or digital album dedicated to these positive moments. Include photos from different stages of their life, focusing on times of joy and connection. Write down funny stories or endearing habits that made them unique. These tangible reminders help anchor our thoughts in the fullness of their life rather than just its end.

Practice conscious thought redirection when negative patterns emerge. When you catch yourself thinking "I should have noticed the symptoms sooner," try shifting to "I gave them a life filled with love and care." Replace "I wish I had more time" with "I'm grateful for every moment we shared."

This isn't about denying the pain or difficulty of loss. Rather, it's about expanding our perspective to include the entire story of our relationship with our pet. By actively choosing to focus on positive memories, we honor their life while supporting our own healing process.

Reflection

The journey of reframing our thoughts after pet loss isn't about erasing pain or pretending everything is fine. Instead, it's about finding balance in our memories and giving ourselves permission to remember the joy alongside the sorrow. When we consciously shift our perspective, we create space for healing while honoring the full spectrum of our relationship with our beloved companions.

This process takes time and patience. Some days, the weight of "what-ifs" may feel overwhelming, while other days bring smiles as we recall a funny moment or cherished routine. Both experiences are valid parts of our healing journey.

Remember that your pet's life was more than their final moments. They were a source of joy, comfort, and unconditional love. By choosing to focus on these positive aspects, we keep their spirit alive in our hearts while gradually releasing the burden of regret.

As you move forward, be gentle with yourself. There's no timeline for healing, and no "right way" to remember. Allow your memories to surface naturally, and when difficult thoughts arise, practice redirecting them toward moments of connection and happiness.

Your pet's legacy lives on through the love you shared and the lessons they taught you. By reframing your thoughts, you honor not just their memory, but also the profound impact they had on your life. This shift in perspective doesn't diminish your loss - it enriches your remembrance with the fullness of your shared journey.

CHAPTER 6

UNDERSTANDING EUTHANASIA: A COMPASSIONATE CHOICE

In the depths of Max's amber eyes, I saw the unwavering loyalty that had been my constant companion for over a decade. As his breathing grew labored and his once-vibrant spirit dimmed, I knew the kindest choice was the most heartbreaking one.

Euthanasia was never a decision I wanted to make, but it was the selfless act of love that Max deserved. Despite the ache in my chest, I couldn't bear to see him suffer any longer. The veterinarian's gentle reassurance did little to ease the guilt that weighed heavily upon me as I stroked his soft fur one final time.

In those last moments, I whispered promises of endless fields and endless treats, wishing I could take his pain upon myself. When his eyes finally closed, a piece of my heart went with him, forever changed by the depth of our bond. Euthanasia was a compassionate release, but that didn't make letting go any easier.

A Final Act of Love

Making end-of-life decisions for our pets ranks among the most challenging responsibilities we face as pet guardians. While natural death remains a possibility, many pet owners will eventually confront the difficult choice of euthanasia. The word itself - derived from Greek meaning "good death" - speaks to its fundamental purpose: preventing unnecessary suffering.

Veterinarians approach these conversations with deep empathy, understanding the gravity of such decisions. During consultations, they assess multiple factors including quality of life, pain levels, and treatment options. They provide medical insights while acknowledging that you know your pet's personality and daily life better than anyone.

A thorough veterinary consultation typically covers several key areas. Your vet will explain your pet's current condition, prognosis, and available treatments. They'll discuss observable signs of pain or distress, helping you understand what your pet is experiencing. Many veterinarians use quality of life scales, which evaluate factors like mobility, appetite, and engagement with family members.

These discussions aren't meant to push you toward a particular choice. Instead, they aim to equip you with clear, honest information so you can make an informed decision aligned with your pet's best interests. Veterinarians often encourage asking questions and taking time to process the information.

Some pet owners find comfort in seeking second opinions or consulting with multiple veterinary professionals. This is completely acceptable and can help affirm that you're making the most appropriate choice for your pet's situation. Veterinarians understand this need for certainty and generally support reaching out to colleagues for additional perspectives.

The decision-making process may span days or weeks, depending on your pet's condition. During this time, your veterinary team can provide guidance on pain management and comfort care, ensuring your pet remains as comfortable as possible while you evaluate options.

Remember that consulting with veterinarians doesn't commit you to any particular course of action. These conversations serve to prepare you with knowledge and understanding, allowing you to make choices from a place of love and informed compassion rather than fear or uncertainty.

Guilt Surrounding Euthanasia

Guilt often emerges as one of the heaviest burdens for pet owners who choose euthanasia. Even when made with careful consideration and deep love, this decision can lead to persistent doubts and self-questioning. These feelings are a natural part of the grieving process, yet understanding their source can help us process them more effectively.

The question of timing weighs particularly heavy. Many pet owners torture themselves with thoughts of "too soon" or "too late." This stems from our deep desire to protect our pets from both suffering and premature death. We want to give them every possible chance while ensuring they don't endure unnecessary pain.

The truth is, there rarely exists a perfect moment for such a decision. Each pet's situation differs, and various factors influence the timing - from medical conditions to quality of life considerations. What matters most is that the decision came from a place of love and the desire to prevent suffering.

Some pet owners experience guilt about feeling relief after their pet's passing. This relief - whether from ending their pet's suffering or from the emotional toll of caregiving - doesn't diminish the love you had for your pet. It's possible to simultaneously feel grief for your loss and relief that your pet is no longer in pain.

These feelings may intensify when we replay the final days or moments in our minds. We might question every detail: Could we have done something differently? Should we have waited longer? Did we act too hastily? This mental replay often distorts our perception of events, making it crucial to remember that we made the best decision possible with the information available at the time.

Working through euthanasia-related guilt requires acknowledging these feelings without letting them overwhelm us. Consider writing down your thoughts about the decision-making process, including the factors that led to your choice. This can help provide perspective and remind you of the careful consideration that went into your decision.

Remember that choosing euthanasia often represents the final act of love we can offer our pets - sparing them from prolonged suffering. While the decision may always carry emotional weight, it doesn't mean you made the wrong choice.

Reassurance About The Decision Making Process

Making the decision to end a pet's suffering through euthanasia represents one of the most profound expressions of love we can offer. While this choice often leaves us questioning ourselves, it's essential to recognize that these decisions typically come from a place of deep compassion and understanding of our pet's needs.

Finding peace with this decision involves acknowledging several key truths. First, our pets rely on us to make difficult choices on their behalf. They cannot tell us directly when they're ready to go, but they often communicate through subtle changes in behavior, appetite, and engagement with life. By paying attention to these signals and consulting with veterinary professionals, we make informed decisions based on our pet's quality of life rather than our desire to keep them with us longer.

Many pet owners find solace in creating a detailed timeline of their pet's condition leading up to the decision. This practice helps provide clarity about the progression of illness or decline, offering concrete evidence that supports the timing of their choice. It can serve as a reminder that the decision wasn't made hastily or without careful consideration.

Others find peace through support groups where they can share their experiences with those who've faced similar choices. Hearing stories from others who've struggled with and ultimately found acceptance of their decisions can provide validation and perspective.

Establishing a ritual or memorial can also help transform feelings of guilt into expressions of gratitude. This might involve creating a photo album of happy memories, writing a letter to your pet expressing your love and reasons for your choice, or planting a tree in their memory. These actions shift focus from the final decision to the entirety of your shared journey.

Remember that choosing euthanasia often prevents unnecessary suffering. While natural death might seem like the kinder option, it can lead to prolonged pain and distress. By making this difficult choice, you've taken on the emotional burden to spare your pet from physical suffering - a selfless act of love.

Support Resources for Those Considering Euthanasia

When facing the difficult decision of euthanasia, you don't have to navigate this challenging path alone. Professional support networks exist specifically to help pet owners through this process, offering guidance, understanding, and practical advice.

Veterinary counselors specialize in end-of-life discussions and can provide valuable insights into your pet's condition. These professionals understand both the medical aspects and the emotional complexity of the situation. They can help evaluate quality of life factors, explain what to expect during the procedure, and address specific concerns about timing or alternatives.

Many veterinary practices now offer dedicated consultation sessions focused solely on end-of-life decisions. During these appointments, you can discuss your pet's specific circumstances without feeling rushed. These conversations often help clarify whether euthanasia is the appropriate choice and, if so, when.

Support groups specifically focused on euthanasia decisions provide a unique space to connect with others facing similar choices. These groups, available both online and in-person, offer forums where you can share concerns, ask questions, and learn from others' experiences. Members often discuss how they knew it was time, what factors influenced their decision, and how they found peace afterward.

Local animal hospitals and humane societies frequently maintain lists of pet loss counselors and support groups. These resources often include:

- Quality of life assessment tools

- Checklists for evaluating your pet's comfort

- Contact information for home euthanasia services

- Referrals to pet hospice programs

Organizations like the Association for Pet Loss and Bereavement (APLB) provide 24/7 chat rooms and scheduled support sessions. These platforms allow you to connect with trained volunteers who understand the complexity of end-of-life decisions and can provide emotional support during the decision-making process.

Remember that seeking support isn't a sign of weakness - it's a reflection of the depth of your love for your pet and your commitment to making the most informed, compassionate decision possible.

Reflection

The decision to euthanize a beloved pet ranks among life's most challenging moments. While no resource can completely eliminate the emotional weight of this choice, understanding and utilizing available support systems can provide clarity and comfort during this difficult time.

Professional guidance serves as a cornerstone of support, offering both medical expertise and emotional understanding. Veterinary counselors and pet loss specialists stand ready to help navigate the complex factors involved in end-of-life decisions. Their experience can help transform overwhelming uncertainty into informed choices based on your pet's specific needs and circumstances.

Support groups and online communities create spaces where pet owners can share their experiences without judgment. These connections remind us that others have walked this path before, offering perspectives that can illuminate our own decision-making process. Through these shared experiences, many find the strength to face difficult choices with greater confidence and peace of mind.

Quality of life assessment tools, provided by veterinary professionals and animal welfare organizations, offer concrete frameworks for evaluating your pet's condition. These resources help transform gut-wrenching uncertainty into clearer understanding, allowing for decisions based on observable factors rather than fear or doubt.

Remember that seeking support reflects the depth of love and responsibility you feel toward your pet. Each resource - whether professional guidance, peer support, or practical tools - exists to honor that bond and help ensure your pet's final chapter reflects the care and dignity they deserve.

By reaching out to these support networks, you gain allies in making one of life's most profound decisions. Though the choice remains deeply personal, you need not face it alone.

CHAPTER 7

FORGIVING YOURSELF: STEPS TOWARD SELF-COMPASSION

The memories of Max's final days still linger vividly. His labored breathing, the dull look in those once vibrant eyes – it's seared into my mind's eye. In those heart-wrenching moments, doubt crept in, questioning if I had done enough, if the timing was right. Had I been selfish, keeping him around for my own comfort while he suffered?

Yet, as time passed, I learned to silence those insidious whispers of regret. Max's love was a gift, one I cherished until the very end. The decision to let him go, as agonizing as it was, came from that same wellspring of love. I didn't withhold his peace out of selfishness but out of a desire to savor every precious moment we had left together.

Our journey's final miles were fraught with hardship, but I know now that I walked them with courage, compassion, and Max's own gentle spirit as my guide. In honoring his life by easing his suffering, I gave him the greatest gift of all – the gift of a love that transcends this mortal world. For that, there can be no regret, only gratitude for the bond we shared.

The Path to Self-Forgiveness

The journey through pet loss carries an often-overlooked burden - the weight of self-judgment. In the aftermath of losing a beloved companion, many find themselves trapped in cycles of harsh self-criticism, replaying decisions and questioning their choices. This internal struggle can anchor us in grief, preventing the natural progression toward healing.

Self-forgiveness emerges as a critical component of the grieving process. Just as we extend compassion to others facing loss, we must learn to direct that same gentle understanding inward. This doesn't mean dismissing our feelings or pretending mistakes weren't made. Rather, it involves acknowledging our humanity and accepting that we acted with the best information and intentions available at the time.

Consider starting each day with a moment of self-compassion meditation. Find a quiet space, place your hand over your heart, and breathe deeply. Acknowledge your pain without judgment: "I'm hurting because I loved deeply." This simple practice can help soften the sharp edges of self-criticism.

Affirmations serve as powerful tools for rewiring negative thought patterns. Create personal statements that resonate with your experience:

"I made decisions out of love and care for my pet."

"I honor the relationship we shared by being gentle with myself."

"I release the burden of perfect decisions and embrace my humanity."

Write these affirmations where you'll see them daily - on mirrors, in journals, or as phone reminders. Speaking them aloud adds another layer of impact, helping to internalize these messages of self-compassion.

The practice of letter-writing offers another path toward self-forgiveness. Write to yourself from your pet's perspective, expressing the unconditional love they showed during your time together. This exercise often reveals the disconnect between how harshly we judge ourselves and the pure acceptance our pets always offered.

Remember that self-forgiveness isn't a destination but a practice. Some days will feel easier than others. When you notice self-criticism arising, pause and ask:

"Would I speak this way to a friend going through the same situation?" This simple question often illuminates the disparity between the compassion we offer others and the judgment we reserve for ourselves.

Practical Exercises for Self-Forgiveness

Healing requires active engagement with our emotions. The following exercises offer structured ways to cultivate self-forgiveness and process your grief journey.

Loving-Kindness Meditation

Find a comfortable position and close your eyes. Begin with three deep breaths, allowing your body to settle. Picture your pet in a moment of joy - perhaps playing in the sunlight or curled up beside you. Now, direct these phrases toward yourself:

"May I be gentle with myself during this time of grief"

"May I remember the love we shared"

"May I find peace in the choices I made"

"May I forgive myself as completely as my pet loved me"

Repeat these phrases a few times and let them sink into your consciousness.

Daily Journaling Practice

Set aside 15 minutes each day for reflective writing. These prompts can guide your exploration:

- What decision am I struggling to forgive myself for?

- What would my pet say about this situation?

- How did I show love and care throughout our relationship?

- What did I learn from this experience that makes me a more compassionate person?

Write without judgment or editing. Let your thoughts flow naturally onto the page.

<u>Gratitude and Release Exercise</u>

Create two columns on a piece of paper. In the first column, list moments you're grateful for from your time with your pet. In the second, write down the regrets or decisions you're ready to release. After completing both lists, read them aloud. Then tear off the regrets column and either burn it safely or tear it into tiny pieces - a physical representation of letting go.

<u>Mirror Work</u>

Stand before a mirror each morning. Look into your own eyes and speak these words:

"I made decisions based on love"

"I gave my pet a life filled with care"

"I release the burden of perfect choices"

"I deserve compassion and understanding"

This exercise might feel uncomfortable at first. Start with just one minute and gradually increase the duration as you become more comfortable with self-compassion.

Barriers to Self-Forgiveness

Many pet owners find themselves trapped in cycles of guilt, unable to move forward due to internal and external barriers that block the path to self-forgiveness. Understanding these obstacles marks the first step toward dismantling them.

One significant barrier stems from the fear that forgiving ourselves means forgetting our pets. This manifests in thoughts like "If I stop feeling guilty, I'm betraying their memory" or "My guilt proves how much I loved them." This mindset creates a false connection between remembrance and self-punishment. In reality, releasing guilt opens space for more meaningful ways to honor your pet's memory through joy and celebration of their life.

Personal belief systems about responsibility and perfection create additional roadblocks. Those who pride themselves on being excellent caregivers may struggle to reconcile perceived failures in their pet's final days. The myth of perfect pet ownership - that we should somehow predict or prevent every possible issue - sets an impossible standard that no one can meet.

Some pet owners hold onto guilt as a form of self-punishment, believing they don't deserve peace after making difficult end-of-life decisions. This mentality often connects to deeper patterns of self-criticism that extend beyond pet loss. Recognizing these patterns helps separate legitimate grief from habitual self-judgment.

Religious or spiritual beliefs can also impact self-forgiveness. Some traditions view animals differently than humans, leading to confusion about how to process pet loss within one's faith framework. Others may worry about questions of afterlife or whether they'll reunite with their pets, adding another layer of complexity to their grief.

These barriers, while significant, are not insurmountable. Awareness of these obstacles allows us to approach them with compassion and develop strategies to move beyond them.

Reflection

Moving past barriers to self-forgiveness requires both patience and dedication. Like any journey of emotional healing, it begins with small steps and builds momentum over time. While these obstacles may feel overwhelming at first, understanding their nature makes them less intimidating and more manageable.

The path to self-forgiveness opens when we recognize that guilt serves no constructive purpose in honoring our pets' memories. Our beloved companions gave us unconditional love - they would never want us to suffer endless self-recrimination. They lived in the present moment, finding joy in simple pleasures and our company. Perhaps the greatest tribute we can offer is to learn from their example.

Self-forgiveness doesn't mean forgetting or diminishing the significance of our loss. Instead, it creates space for more meaningful ways to remember and celebrate the time we shared. By releasing the weight of guilt, we free ourselves to focus on the countless positive memories and lessons our pets brought into our lives.

Remember that you made the best decisions you could with the information available at the time. No one can predict every outcome or prevent every misfortune. Accepting our human limitations isn't a sign of failure - it's an acknowledgment of reality and a step toward healing.

The barriers to self-forgiveness may feel solid, but they're not permanent. With compassion, support, and gentle persistence, you can move beyond guilt toward a place of peace. Your pet's legacy deserves to be one of love and joy, not endless self-reproach.

CHAPTER 8

JOURNALING FOR HEALING: WRITING THROUGH GRIEF

The rhythmic tapping of my pen against the leather-bound journal had become a familiar companion in the weeks following Max's passing. Each day, I would retreat to the solitude of my study, the faint scent of old books mingling with the aroma of the chamomile tea that had become a ritual of sorts. As I allowed the soothing warmth of the mug to envelop my hands, I would open the journal, its worn pages a testament to the countless words that had spilled forth.

In those early days, the entries were raw, unfiltered outpourings of grief. Sentences blurred together as tears stained the paper, the pain of loss manifesting in jagged scribbles that captured the depths of my anguish. But with each passing day, something shifted. The sharp edges of sorrow began to soften, and the words took on a gentler cadence, weaving tales of cherished memories and the profound impact Max had on my life.

Finding Healing Through Writing

In times of grief, our thoughts and emotions can feel like a tangled web inside our minds. Writing offers a powerful way to unravel these complex feelings, bringing clarity and relief through the simple act of putting pen to paper.

Journaling creates a private sanctuary where you can express your deepest emotions about your pet's loss without judgment or restraint. Unlike conversations, which require immediate responses, writing allows you to pause, reflect, and explore your feelings at your own pace. The blank page becomes a patient listener, ready to receive whatever thoughts emerge.

Free-writing serves as a particularly effective method. Set aside a few minutes each day to write continuously, without editing or censoring yourself. Let your thoughts flow naturally, even if they seem disconnected or raw. You might start by describing a cherished memory of your pet, only to find yourself processing feelings of anger or guilt. This stream-of-consciousness approach often reveals emotions you didn't realize you were carrying.

Structured prompts can also guide your exploration. Consider questions like:

- What made your pet's personality unique?

- What lessons did your pet teach you about love and companionship?

- What moments of joy do you remember most vividly?

Gratitude-focused journaling helps shift perspective while honoring your pet's memory. Each entry might begin with "Today I'm grateful for..." followed by specific aspects of your relationship with your pet. These could include simple things like the sound of their purring, the way they greeted you after work, or how they made you laugh during difficult times.

The physical act of writing engages both mind and body in the healing process. Whether you prefer a leather-bound journal or a simple notebook, the tactile experience of writing by hand can feel more intimate and therapeutic than typing on a device. Your journal becomes a tangible record of your journey through grief, documenting not just your pain but also your gradual steps toward healing.

Remember that your journal is yours alone. There's no need to write perfectly or follow strict rules. Some days might bring pages of detailed memories, while others might hold just a few words or even tear stains. Each entry represents another small step in your healing journey.

Guided Journaling Exercises

To help structure your writing practice, try these focused exercises designed to explore specific aspects of your grief journey. Take your time with each prompt, allowing yourself to fully process the emotions that arise.

Letter to Your Pet

Begin by writing a heartfelt letter to your pet. Find a quiet space where you feel comfortable expressing your deepest feelings. Start with "Dear [pet's name]" and let your words flow naturally. Share the thoughts you wish you could tell them - your love, your regrets, your gratitude. Tell them about your life now and how you're coping with their absence. Express what you miss most about them and the dreams you had for your future together.

Consider these reflection questions to deepen your letter:

- What did I learn from our time together?

- What do I wish we could experience one more time?

- How has my life changed since you've been gone?

- What would I want you to know about how much you meant to me?

Exploring Loss and Resilience

Use these prompts to examine your grief journey and personal growth:

1. Describe the moment you felt strongest in your grief. What gave you strength?

2. What has surprised you most about your grieving process?

3. How has this loss changed your perspective on life and love?

4. What coping strategies have helped you most?

5. Where do you find comfort when memories feel overwhelming?

6. What would you tell someone else going through a similar loss?

Memory Timeline Exercise

Create a timeline of significant moments with your pet. Include:

- First meeting/adoption day

- Memorable adventures together

- Funny habits or quirks

- Special traditions you shared

- Important milestones

- Final days and moments

For each memory, write about:

- The emotions you felt then

- How these memories make you feel now

- What these moments taught you about love and companionship

Creativity in Journaling

While traditional journaling focuses on written expression, incorporating artistic elements can unlock deeper emotional connections and memories. Your journal can become more than just words on a page - it can transform into a vibrant tribute to your beloved pet.

Consider adding sketches alongside your written entries. These don't need to be masterpieces - even simple line drawings can capture essential memories. Draw your pet's favorite sleeping spot, their characteristic head tilt, or that special toy they carried everywhere. The act of drawing slows down your thought process, allowing you to notice details you might have forgotten: the exact pattern of spots on their fur, the way their tail curled when happy, or their unique facial expressions.

Photos add another powerful dimension to your grief journal. Include snapshots from different stages of your pet's life - their first day home, holiday celebrations, lazy afternoon naps, or adventures in the park. Write about the stories behind these images. What was happening just before or after the photo was taken? What emotions surface when you look at them now?

Create memory collages by combining photos with physical mementos. Consider including:

- A piece of their favorite blanket

- Their ID tag or collar

- Pressed flowers from their favorite walking route

- Paw prints preserved in clay

- Cards or notes from sympathetic friends

- Fur clippings saved from grooming sessions

These tactile elements bring a physical connection to your journaling practice. Each item holds its own story and emotional resonance. As you arrange these pieces, you're creating a visual narrative of your shared life together.

Leave space in your journal for unexpected creative inspiration. Some days you might feel drawn to write poetry, other times you might want to paint or sketch. Your grief journal should be flexible enough to accommodate whatever form of expression feels most healing in the moment.

Remember that artistic journaling isn't about creating perfect works of art - it's about expressing your emotions and preserving memories in ways that words alone sometimes cannot capture.

Reflection

Journaling serves as a powerful bridge between grief and healing, offering a private space to process complex emotions and preserve cherished memories. Through the combination of written reflection and artistic expression, your journal becomes more than a record of loss - it transforms into a living memorial that grows and evolves with your healing journey.

The blank pages invite honest exploration of your feelings without judgment. Whether through carefully crafted prose, quick emotional sketches, or lovingly arranged mementos, each entry builds upon the last to create a deeply personal tribute to your pet. This creative process helps move grief from something that feels overwhelming and abstract into tangible form, making it easier to understand and ultimately accept.

Your journal also becomes a touchstone for future moments when you need comfort or want to revisit happy memories. Unlike static memorials, a grief journal remains dynamic - reflecting your changing relationship with loss while preserving the essence of your bond with your pet. The combination of words, images, and physical mementos creates a multi-sensory experience that captures your pet's spirit more fully than any single medium could achieve.

Remember that there's no "right way" to maintain your grief journal. Some days may call for lengthy written reflections, while others might be better served by simple sketches or carefully chosen photographs. Let your emotional needs guide your creative choices, and trust that each entry contributes to your healing process in its own unique way.

Through this creative journaling practice, you honor both your pet's memory and your own grief journey. Each page becomes a testament to the depth of your love and the enduring impact your pet had on your life.

CHAPTER 9

MINDFULNESS PRACTICES: STAYING PRESENT IN THE MOMENT

In the aftermath of Max's passing, I found solace in mindfulness practices that anchored me to the present moment. During those initial days of raw grief, the weight of my loss threatened to consume me entirely. But through simple breathing exercises and guided meditations, I gradually learned to create pockets of stillness amidst the emotional turmoil.

Some days I would sit cross-legged on the floor where Max's bed used to be, closing my eyes and focusing on the gentle rise and fall of my breath. As memories and regrets inevitably surfaced, I gently acknowledged them without judgment, then returned my attention to the steady rhythm within. In those moments of presence, the heaviness in my chest would ease, if only briefly.

Over time, I expanded my mindfulness practice beyond formal meditation. While out on walks I once shared with Max, I made a conscious effort to engage my senses - noticing the crunch of leaves underfoot, the warmth of the sun on my face, the distant calls of birds. These small anchors to the here and now became beacons of solace, reminding me that even in the depths of sorrow, fleeting moments of peace were possible.

Finding Peace Through Mindfulness

In the depths of grief, our minds often spiral between past memories and future worries, making it difficult to find stability in the present moment. Mindfulness offers a gentle anchor, helping us navigate the turbulent waters of loss while honoring our natural grieving process.

Mindfulness doesn't ask us to forget or move on - instead, it creates space to experience our emotions without becoming overwhelmed by them. By focusing on the present moment, we can acknowledge our grief while maintaining a sense of groundedness that supports our healing journey.

Start with simple breathing exercises. Find a quiet spot where you won't be disturbed, perhaps near a window or in your favorite chair. Place one hand on your chest and the other on your belly. Take a deep breath through your nose, feeling your belly expand like a balloon. Hold this breath for a count of three, then release it slowly through your mouth. Notice how your body naturally relaxes with each exhale. Continue this pattern for five minutes, gradually increasing the duration as you become more comfortable with the practice.

Body scan meditations offer another powerful tool for releasing grief-related tension. Lie down in a comfortable position and close your eyes. Beginning with your toes, bring your attention to each part of your body in sequence. Notice any areas where you're holding stress or emotion - perhaps tension in your shoulders or a heaviness in your chest. Don't try to change these sensations; simply observe them with gentle awareness. As you progress through the scan, imagine each breath carrying soothing energy to these areas of discomfort.

These practices might feel challenging at first, especially when grief feels raw. You may experience tears or strong emotions during meditation - this is completely normal and even beneficial. Consider these moments as your body's natural way of processing loss. Start with short sessions of just a few minutes and gradually extend them as you build comfort with the practice.

Simple Mindfulness Exercises

Let's explore some simple mindfulness practices you can incorporate into your daily routine to help process your grief and find moments of peace.

Guided Imagery Exercise: Finding Comfort in Memories

1. Find a quiet space and settle into a comfortable position

2. Take three deep breaths to center yourself

3. Picture a favorite moment with your pet - perhaps a sunny afternoon in the backyard or a cozy evening on the couch

4. Notice the details: the warmth of their fur, the sound of their breathing, the way they moved

5. Stay with this memory for 5-10 minutes, allowing yourself to fully experience the positive emotions it brings

6. When ready, slowly open your eyes and take a moment to appreciate this connection

Walking Meditation Practice:

1. Choose a peaceful location - a park, garden, or quiet neighborhood

2. Begin walking at a slower pace than usual

3. Focus on the physical sensations - your feet touching the ground, the rhythm of your steps

4. Notice the environment around you - trees swaying, birds singing, the feel of the breeze

5. When memories of your pet arise, acknowledge them gently

6. If emotions surface, pause and take a few deep breaths

7. Continue walking, maintaining awareness of your surroundings and

physical sensations

8. Practice for 10-15 minutes initially, extending the duration as comfortable

These exercises work best when practiced regularly. Start with just a few minutes each day, gradually increasing the duration as you become more comfortable with the practice. Remember there's no "right" way to do these exercises - your experience will be unique to you and your grief journey.

Both practices can help ground you in the present moment while creating space to honor your pet's memory in a gentle, nurturing way. The key is consistency rather than perfection.

Mindfulness in Grief Management

Mindfulness offers powerful tools for managing the intense emotions that accompany pet loss. By practicing present-moment awareness, you can create a gentle space to process your grief while preventing overwhelming emotional spirals.

The simple act of focused breathing serves as an anchor during turbulent moments. When memories of your pet trigger waves of sadness or anxiety, pause and direct your attention to your breath. Notice the natural rhythm of your inhales and exhales without trying to change them. This brings your nervous system back into balance, reducing the physical symptoms of stress like racing thoughts or a tight chest.

Mindfulness also helps build emotional resilience by teaching us to observe our feelings without judgment. Rather than pushing away painful emotions about your pet's loss, practice acknowledging them with compassion. When grief arises, try naming the emotion: "I'm feeling sadness" or "This is anxiety." This small step of recognition often diminishes the emotion's overwhelming power.

The practice enhances our capacity to stay present with difficult feelings instead of avoiding them. Many grieving pet owners find themselves caught between wanting to remember their companion and fearing the pain those memories bring. Mindfulness creates a middle path - allowing us to honor our pet's memory while maintaining emotional balance.

Through regular mindfulness practice, you'll develop greater awareness of your grief patterns. You may notice certain times of day or specific triggers that intensify your emotions. This understanding lets you prepare supportive strategies in advance, like scheduling quiet reflection time or reaching out to understanding friends.

Most importantly, mindfulness cultivates acceptance - not of the loss itself, but of your natural grieving process. There's no timeline for healing, and mindfulness helps us meet each moment as it comes. Some days will feel lighter, others heavier. The practice teaches us to hold both experiences with equal care and patience.

Remember that building mindfulness skills takes time. Start with short periods of practice and gradually extend them as you feel ready. Even a few mindful breaths can create valuable space between intense emotions and your response to them.

Mindfulness Tools

In today's digital age, technology can be a valuable ally in developing your mindfulness practice. Many apps offer guided meditations specifically designed for grief and emotional healing, making it easier to establish a consistent routine.

Popular apps like Headspace and Calm provide structured programs that guide you through the basics of mindfulness meditation. These apps offer bite-sized sessions, perfect for beginners who might feel overwhelmed by longer practices. Look for meditation series focused on grief, loss, or emotional processing - these often include gentle guidance tailored to your experience.

The Insight Timer app hosts an extensive library of free meditations led by experienced teachers. You'll find specific sessions addressing pet loss, along with practices for managing anxiety and cultivating self-compassion. The app's timer feature also supports silent meditation, allowing you to set gentle bells at intervals that help maintain focus.

Online workshops and classes provide deeper exploration of mindfulness techniques. Platforms like Coursera and Udemy offer structured courses on mindfulness-based stress reduction (MBSR), which can be particularly helpful during the grieving process. These courses often include video instruction, guided practices, and community support through discussion forums.

Many grief counselors and pet loss support groups now offer virtual mindfulness sessions. These specialized classes create safe spaces to practice mindfulness while connecting with others who understand your experience. Check with local veterinary clinics or pet loss support organizations for recommendations.

YouTube channels dedicated to mindfulness meditation provide free, accessible content you can access anytime. Search for guided visualizations that incorporate memories of your pet, or find body scan meditations to release physical tension carried from grief.

Consider setting up mindfulness reminders on your phone. Apps like Mind-Bell or Mindfulness Bell chime at random or set intervals throughout the day, prompting you to pause and take a few conscious breaths. These gentle interruptions help maintain awareness and prevent getting lost in overwhelming thoughts about your loss.

Remember to approach these digital tools with patience. Experiment with different apps and formats until you find what resonates with your personal practice. The goal isn't to achieve perfect meditation - it's to develop sustainable habits that support your healing journey.

Reflection

In embracing mindfulness through digital tools and resources, you open new pathways for healing and self-discovery. These technological aids serve as companions on your grief journey, offering structured support when you need it most. While no app or online course can erase the pain of losing a beloved pet, these resources provide valuable frameworks for processing emotions and finding moments of peace.

The key is to approach these tools with gentle curiosity and self-compassion. Start small - perhaps with a five-minute guided meditation or a single mindful breath when your phone chimes. Allow yourself to explore different options without pressure to maintain a perfect practice. Some days, you might find comfort in a lengthy meditation session; other days, a few conscious breaths might be all you can manage. Both are equally valid expressions of mindfulness.

Remember that these digital resources complement, rather than replace, your personal healing process. They offer guidance and structure while honoring the unique nature of your grief journey. Whether through an app's gentle reminders, an online community's shared experiences, or a virtual workshop's structured learning, each tool adds another layer of support to your mindfulness practice.

As you continue exploring these resources, stay attuned to what serves you best. Your needs may change as you move through different phases of grief. The flexibility of digital tools allows you to adapt your practice accordingly, always returning to what feels most nurturing and supportive in the present moment.

Let these mindfulness resources be anchors in times of emotional turbulence, helping you stay grounded while honoring your pet's memory. Through consistent, gentle practice, you'll develop a deeper capacity for presence and self-awareness - essential qualities that support healing and growth after loss.

CHAPTER 10

HANDLING INSENSITIVE COMMENTS: RESPONDING WITH GRACE

The insensitive comments began soon after Max's passing. Well-meaning friends and family tried to console me, but their words often stung more than soothed.

"He was just a dog, you know. You can always get another one."

Those casual remarks minimized the profound bond I shared with Max, as if he were merely an object to be replaced. They failed to grasp how he had been an integral part of my life, a constant companion through thick and thin.

"Aren't you overreacting a bit? It's been weeks already."

The assumption that grief follows a rigid timeline only added to my frustration. Healing doesn't adhere to societal expectations or tidy schedules. The enormity of Max's absence was a void that couldn't be filled overnight.

Even those closest to me struggled to understand the depths of my sorrow. "You'll get over it eventually. Just stay busy and it'll get easier."

While intended as encouragement, such platitudes dismissed the validity of my pain. Grief demanded space for reflection, not mere distraction. Staying busy might numb the ache temporarily, but it couldn't facilitate true healing.

Dealing with Insensitive Comments

The path through pet loss often becomes more challenging when we encounter well-meaning but hurtful remarks from others. Comments like "It was just a dog" or "You can always get another cat" pierce deeply into our grieving hearts, yet these statements remain surprisingly common in our society.

Understanding why people make such remarks helps us navigate these painful interactions. Many individuals who haven't experienced the profound bond with an animal companion simply cannot grasp the depth of our loss. Their frame of reference lacks the daily rituals, the unconditional love, and the years of shared experiences that define our relationships with our pets.

Cultural perspectives also shape how others respond to pet loss. In some societies, animals serve purely utilitarian purposes - as working animals or property rather than family members. These deeply ingrained beliefs influence how people view the grieving process for pets. Someone raised in a culture where animals live outdoors and serve specific functions might struggle to understand mourning what they view as "just a pet."

This disconnect often stems from traditional grieving customs that focus exclusively on human loss. Many cultures lack established rituals or protocols for acknowledging pet death, leaving people uncertain how to respond when someone loses an animal companion. Without clear social guidelines, they may default to dismissive statements or attempt to "fix" your grief with quick solutions.

The generation gap can also play a role. Older family members might have grown up in an era when pets were considered replaceable and emotional attachments to animals were discouraged. Their attempts to help may reflect outdated attitudes about pet relationships rather than intentional insensitivity.

Even within families that cherish pets, individuals process loss differently. A person who copes through immediate action might push you to "get another pet" without recognizing your need to mourn. Their suggestion comes from wanting to ease your pain, though it may feel invalidating to your grief.

Graceful Responses

When faced with insensitive comments, responding with grace not only preserves relationships but also protects our emotional well-being. Here are effective strategies to handle these challenging interactions:

Use "I" statements to express your feelings without accusation. Instead of reacting with anger when someone suggests "getting over it," try saying "I'm still processing this loss and need time to grieve." This approach acknowledges your emotions while avoiding confrontation.

Frame your response as an opportunity for education. "My pet was a family member who brought joy to my life for fifteen years. Their absence leaves a significant void." This helps others understand the depth of your connection without becoming defensive.

Sometimes, a simple acknowledgment followed by a subject change works best. When someone makes an inappropriate comparison between pet and human loss, respond with "Everyone grieves differently" and shift the conversation to a shared interest or neutral topic.

Practice prepared responses for common insensitive remarks. Having these ready helps maintain composure in difficult moments:

"I appreciate your concern, but I need to process this in my own way."

"Thank you for trying to help. Right now, I just need someone to listen."

"I understand you might see this differently, but this loss is significant to me."

Set boundaries when needed. If someone repeatedly makes dismissive comments, it's acceptable to say "I find those comments hurtful. Could we please avoid discussing this topic?"

Remember that maintaining grace under pressure doesn't mean suppressing your feelings. Find appropriate outlets for processing your emotions after these encounters, whether through journaling, talking with understanding friends, or consulting your grief counselor.

Consider timing when addressing insensitive remarks. Sometimes, waiting until you're less emotional allows for more productive conversations about why certain comments feel hurtful.

Empathy and Education

While responding with grace protects our emotional well-being, these moments also present opportunities to educate others about the profound impact of pet loss. The key lies in approaching these conversations with patience and understanding.

When someone dismisses your grief, share a specific memory that illustrates your bond. "Murphy wasn't just a dog - he waited by the door every day when I came home from chemotherapy treatments. His presence helped me through the darkest times of my life." Personal stories humanize the experience and help others understand the depth of the connection.

Studies have shown that the grief experienced after losing a pet can be as intense as losing a human family member. The American Veterinary Medical Association recognizes that pet loss can trigger clinical depression, anxiety, and even symptoms of post-traumatic stress disorder. Sharing these facts helps validate the experience of pet loss grief.

Consider explaining how pets integrate into our daily routines and emotional lives. "My cat Sophie was part of every morning for sixteen years. She sat with me during breakfast, kept me company while I worked, and curled up next to me every night. That's thousands of moments of connection that suddenly disappeared."

Frame the conversation around universal experiences of love and loss. Most people understand the pain of losing someone they love, even if they haven't experienced pet loss specifically. Draw parallels that help them relate: "Just like you treasure photos of loved ones, I keep pictures of Bailey because she was family to me."

Remember that education doesn't mean defending your grief. Instead, focus on building bridges of understanding. Share resources from veterinary organizations or grief counselors that explain the science behind human-animal bonds. This approach shifts the conversation from personal judgment to documented research and professional perspectives.

When discussing the impact on mental health, be honest about the healing process. "Working through this grief with a counselor helped me understand how deeply pets affect our emotional well-being. Did you know that many therapists now specialize in pet loss because of its significant psychological impact?"

Maintaining Composure During Difficult Conversations

Staying composed when faced with insensitive comments about pet loss requires both emotional awareness and practical techniques. By developing these skills, we protect our well-being while preserving meaningful relationships.

Deep breathing serves as an immediate anchor during challenging conversations. Before responding to dismissive remarks, take three slow breaths. Inhale through your nose for a count of four, hold for two, then exhale through your mouth for six counts. This simple practice activates your parasympathetic nervous system, reducing stress hormones and allowing your rational mind to guide your response.

Mindfulness techniques help maintain emotional balance. Ground yourself by focusing on physical sensations - feel your feet on the floor, notice the temperature of the air, or touch a smooth stone or comfort object in your pocket. These tactile connections to the present moment prevent emotional overwhelm and reactive responses.

Consider practicing the STOP method:

- Stop what you're doing

- Take a breath

- Observe your thoughts and feelings

- Proceed mindfully

This brief pause creates space between the trigger and your response, allowing you to choose your words with intention rather than reacting from hurt.

Body language plays a crucial role in maintaining composure. Keep your shoulders relaxed, uncross your arms, and maintain a neutral facial expression. These physical adjustments not only project calmness but actually help regulate your emotional state through the mind-body connection.

Remember that maintaining composure doesn't mean suppressing emotions. Instead, it means channeling feelings into constructive responses. You might say, "I appreciate that you may not understand, but my grief is real and valid." This acknowledges your feelings while setting clear boundaries.

Preparation helps maintain equilibrium. Consider rehearsing calm responses to common dismissive comments. Having these gentle but firm replies ready reduces anxiety and increases confidence in difficult conversations.

Regular self-care practices strengthen emotional resilience. Daily meditation, even for five minutes, builds the mental muscles needed for composure. Physical exercise releases tension that might otherwise surface during triggering conversations.

Reflection

Maintaining composure during difficult conversations about pet loss requires practice, patience, and self-compassion. While challenging, these skills prove invaluable not only in navigating grief but in fostering understanding within our communities.

The techniques discussed - from mindful breathing to prepared responses - form a toolkit for managing emotional reactions while honoring our pets' memories. By remaining composed, we create opportunities for meaningful dialogue about the profound impact of pet loss.

Remember that staying composed doesn't mean denying your feelings or accepting dismissive attitudes. Rather, it means channeling grief into constructive expressions that validate your experience while maintaining your dignity and peace of mind.

Through mindful responses and gentle education, we can help others understand the depth of the human-animal bond. Each composed interaction plants seeds of empathy, gradually shifting cultural perspectives on pet loss grief.

As you navigate these conversations, trust in your ability to remain centered while staying true to your emotional experience. Your grief is valid, and your composure in the face of misunderstanding demonstrates both strength and wisdom.

CHAPTER 11

GENTLE CONVERSATIONS: EXPLAINING DEATH TO CHILDREN

The morning sun filtered through the curtains, casting a warm glow across the living room. I sat on the couch, flanked by my two children, their eyes wide with curiosity. Taking a deep breath, I began to share the story of Max, our beloved family dog who had been by our side for the last eight years.

"You both know how much Max meant to us," I started, my voice tinged with nostalgia. "From the day we brought him home as a tiny puppy, he became an integral part of our family. He was there for every milestone, every celebration, and every heartache."

I paused, letting the memories wash over me. "Remember how he would greet us at the door, his tail wagging furiously, as if we were the most important people in the world? And how he would curl up next to us on the couch, offering his unwavering companionship and unconditional love?"

My daughter, Emma, nodded solemnly, her eyes glistening with tears. "I miss him so much," she whispered, leaning into my embrace.

"I know, sweetheart," I replied, gently stroking her hair. "Losing Max was one of the hardest things we've ever had to go through as a family. But it's important to remember that the pain we feel is a testament to the incredible bond we shared with him."

I turned to my son, Jack, who had been listening intently. "Max taught us so many valuable lessons about love, loyalty, and living in the moment. He reminded us to appreciate the simple joys in life, like a sunny day or a leisurely walk in the park."

Jack nodded, a faint smile tugging at the corners of his mouth. "Remember how he would chase squirrels in the backyard?" he chuckled, his eyes sparkling with the memory.

"Yes," I laughed, "and how he would come back, looking so proud of himself, even though he never actually caught one."

Helping Children Understand Pet Loss

When a beloved pet dies, parents and caregivers face the additional challenge of helping children process their grief. The death of a pet often marks a child's first encounter with loss, making it a crucial teaching moment that shapes their understanding of mortality and emotional processing.

The instinct to shield children from pain leads many adults to use gentle euphemisms like "went to sleep" or "crossed the rainbow bridge." While well-intentioned, these phrases can create confusion and anxiety in children. A child told their pet "went to sleep" might develop fears about their own bedtime or worry that other family members who go to sleep won't wake up.

Instead, use clear, direct language that leaves no room for misinterpretation. "Buddy died" provides a concrete explanation that, though painful, helps children grasp the reality of the situation. This straightforward approach prevents the additional trauma of misconceptions or false hopes.

When discussing death's permanence, tailor your explanation to the child's developmental stage. A preschooler might need to hear that death means the pet's body stopped working and can't be fixed. An older child may be ready for more detailed discussions about the biological aspects of death.

Consider this example:

"Rover's body stopped working. When animals die, their bodies can't move, eat, or play anymore. They don't feel any pain, but they can't come back to life. It's okay to feel sad and miss them."

This approach:

- States the truth clearly

- Explains death's permanence

- Addresses common concerns about suffering

- Validates emotional responses

Avoid statements like "God needed another angel" or "he's in a better place," which might raise difficult theological questions or suggest the pet chose to leave. Focus instead on the concrete reality while remaining sensitive to your family's spiritual beliefs.

Remember that children often process grief differently than adults. They may appear unaffected one moment and overwhelmed the next. Some might ask repeated questions about death, requiring patient, consistent answers. This repetition helps them gradually understand and accept the loss.

Understanding Children's Developmental Stages

Different age groups require distinct approaches when discussing pet loss. What comforts a toddler may frustrate a teenager, and explanations must evolve with the child's cognitive development.

For children ages 2-4, keep explanations basic and concrete. At this stage, children understand the world through direct experiences and struggle with abstract concepts. Focus on observable changes:

"When pets die, their bodies don't move anymore. They can't eat, play, or breathe. That's why we won't see Fluffy running around the house."

Ages 5-7 begin grasping more complex ideas but still think literally. They may worry death is contagious or believe their thoughts caused the pet's death. Address these concerns directly:

"Spot died because he was very old and sick. It's not because you forgot to feed him once, and you can't catch what he had. Sometimes bodies wear out and stop working, like an old toy that breaks."

Children 8-11 understand death's permanence and may ask specific questions about biological processes. They're ready for more detailed explanations:

"When animals die, their organs stop functioning. The heart doesn't pump blood, the lungs don't take in air, and the brain stops sending signals to the body. This isn't like sleeping - it's permanent."

Teenagers process death similarly to adults but may struggle expressing their emotions. They need space to grieve while knowing support is available:

"I know you and Max were especially close. It's okay if you want to talk about him or prefer being alone. There's no right or wrong way to feel."

Throughout all stages, maintain consistency in your explanations. If multiple adults discuss the loss with the child, ensure everyone uses similar language and concepts. This prevents confusion and helps children build a stable understanding of death and grief.

Remember that children revisit their grief as they mature. A child who seemed to accept the loss at age four may have new questions and emotions at seven. Welcome these discussions as opportunities for deeper understanding and emotional growth.

Promote Open Dialogue for Children's Grief

Children need a supportive environment to process their pet's death. When they feel secure expressing their emotions, healing becomes more natural and complete.

Set aside dedicated time for conversations about the lost pet. This shows children their feelings matter and deserve attention. Create quiet moments before bedtime or during weekend afternoons when you can focus entirely on their needs.

Watch for signs your child wants to talk. They might bring up memories of the pet, ask seemingly unrelated questions about death, or display changes in behavior. These moments offer opportunities to open dialogue:

"I noticed you've been looking at Bella's favorite spot by the window. Would you like to tell me what you're thinking about?"

When children voice difficult emotions, acknowledge them without judgment:

"It makes sense that you're angry. You miss throwing the ball with Rex, and it hurts that he's gone."

Some children express grief through play or art rather than words. Provide materials like crayons, paper, or clay. Let them act out scenarios with toys or draw pictures of their pet. These activities help process complex feelings they might struggle to verbalize.

Questions about death may arise at unexpected moments. A child might ask if their pet was in pain, if they'll see them again, or why death happens. Answer honestly while considering their age and emotional state. If you don't know an answer, admit it:

"That's a thoughtful question about where pets go after they die. Different people have different beliefs about this. What do you think?"

Pay attention to recurring questions. Children often need to hear the same explanations multiple times to fully understand and accept the loss. Each repetition helps them process the information and integrate it into their developing worldview.

Create opportunities for children to honor their pet's memory through activities like:

- Making a photo album

- Writing stories about happy memories

- Creating a memorial garden

- Drawing pictures of their favorite moments together

These projects give children concrete ways to express their love and grief while preserving memories of their pet.

Foster Ongoing Conversations About Pet Loss

Grief doesn't follow a set timeline, especially for children who process emotions differently than adults. Creating regular opportunities for conversation helps children work through their feelings at their own pace. These ongoing discussions prove particularly important as children's understanding of loss evolves.

Mealtimes provide natural moments for sharing. The familiar routine of sitting together creates a safe space where memories and emotions can surface organically. A simple question like "What do you remember most about Buddy today?" can spark meaningful exchanges. These conversations validate that it's normal to think about our pets long after they're gone.

Bedtime offers another ideal window for reflection. The quiet moments before sleep often bring thoughts and feelings to the surface. Children might share dreams about their pet or express worries they've held back during busier parts of the day. Listen without judgment, even if they share the same stories repeatedly - this repetition helps process grief.

Some families find success with dedicated "remembering times." These might include:

- Sunday morning breakfast discussions about favorite pet memories

- Weekly family walks where you share stories about your pet's adventures

- Monthly viewings of pet photos or videos

- Special occasions like birthdays or holidays where you intentionally include memories of your pet

Pay attention to subtle cues that your child wants to talk. They might mention seeing a dog that looks like their former pet or become quiet when passing the pet store. These moments present opportunities to check in and show you're ready to listen whenever they need to share.

Dreams about pets deserve special attention. Children often experience vivid dreams about their departed animals. Rather than dismissing these as "just dreams," treat them as valuable opportunities for discussion. These dreams can provide comfort and help process complex emotions about loss.

Encourage expression through questions like:

- "What was your favorite thing to do with [pet's name] today?"

- "Did you think about [pet's name] at school?"

- "Would you like to tell me about your dream?"

Reassure Children of Ongoing Support and Love

During times of loss, children need consistent reassurance that their world remains secure despite this significant change. While their pet companion is gone, they must know their family's love and support remains unwavering and absolute.

Physical comfort plays a vital role in helping children feel secure during grief. A gentle hug, holding hands during difficult conversations, or simply sitting close together creates a safe space for processing emotions. This physical connection reminds them they're not alone in their sadness:

"Come sit with me. We can look at Buffy's pictures together, and you can tell me your favorite memories whenever you want."

Make it clear that talking about their pet isn't limited to specific times or places. Children should feel free to share memories, ask questions, or express sadness whenever these feelings arise. Whether during breakfast, on the way to school, or before bedtime, maintain an open-door policy for discussions about their pet:

"Even though Tippy isn't here anymore, we can still talk about her anytime you want. Happy memories, sad feelings - all of it matters."

Create daily check-in routines that provide regular opportunities for connection. These moments remind children that support remains constant and available:

"How are you feeling about Duke today? Remember, there's no right or wrong way to feel."

When children know their grief has no expiration date, they're more likely to process their emotions naturally rather than suppressing them. Remind them that missing their pet is normal and that family members share these feelings too:

"I miss hearing Milly's collar jingling in the hallway too. It's okay to feel sad about that. We can miss her together."

Continue to include mentions of the pet in family conversations, showing children that their beloved companion remains part of the family's shared history. This helps normalize ongoing feelings of loss while preserving precious memories:

"Remember how Charlie used to wait by the door when you came home from school? He was such a special part of our family."

Modeling Healthy Grief Expression

As adults, we often feel pressured to maintain composure during difficult times, especially around children. However, when dealing with pet loss, showing our genuine emotions becomes vital for our children's healing process. By expressing our own grief openly, we give children permission to acknowledge and process their feelings.

Share your memories and emotions about your pet naturally. Instead of hiding tears, explain them: "I'm crying because I really miss how Trixie would greet me at the door every evening." This helps children understand that sadness is a normal response to loss and that expressing it helps us heal.

Family meetings can provide structured opportunities for emotional sharing. Create a comfortable routine - perhaps gathering in the living room after dinner or during weekend mornings. Use simple prompts like "Today I remembered..." or "I felt sad when..." to start conversations. Some families pass around a special object, giving each person uninterrupted time to speak.

Consider implementing "feeling circles" where family members take turns expressing their emotions through various methods. This might include:

- Drawing pictures of memories with your pet

- Sharing favorite stories

- Using color cards to represent different emotions

- Playing music that reminds you of your pet

- Writing messages or letters

Remember that children often mirror adult behavior. If you suppress your emotions or dismiss them as unimportant, children may learn to do the same. Instead, demonstrate healthy ways to cope with grief:

- Take deep breaths when feeling overwhelmed

- Use "I feel" statements to express emotions

- Show that it's okay to laugh and share happy memories

- Acknowledge when you need time alone to process feelings

- Seek support from friends or family members

By modeling these behaviors, we teach children valuable emotional skills that extend beyond pet loss, helping them develop resilience and emotional intelligence for future life challenges.

Reflection

Supporting children through pet loss requires a delicate balance of honesty, empathy, and consistent reassurance. While the immediate pain may feel overwhelming for young ones, providing them with the right emotional tools and unwavering support creates a foundation for healthy grief processing.

Children learn valuable life lessons through pet loss - about love, mortality, and the importance of cherishing memories. By maintaining open dialogue and creating safe spaces for emotional expression, we help them develop resilience and emotional intelligence that will serve them throughout their lives.

The key lies in remaining present and attentive to their needs, understanding that each child's grief journey unfolds differently. Some may want to talk constantly about their pet, while others process quietly. Both approaches deserve equal validation and support.

Through consistent comfort and honest communication, we show children that while loss is painful, they never have to face it alone. This security allows them to move through grief at their own pace while maintaining their emotional wellbeing and their cherished memories of their beloved pet companion.

Remember that supporting a grieving child isn't about having all the answers - it's about being there, listening without judgment, and providing the steady presence they need to navigate this challenging experience. With time and patience, children can emerge from pet loss with a deeper understanding of love, loss, and the enduring bonds we share with our animal friends.

CHAPTER 12

STORYTELLING AND ILLUSTRATIONS: HELPING KIDS PROCESS GRIEF

I remember when Max was first diagnosed with lymphoma. My kids, Emma and Jack, were devastated by the news. Emma was only nine at the time, and Jack was twelve. They had grown up with Max as a constant companion, and the thought of losing him was almost too much to bear.

To help them process their grief, I turned to the power of storytelling. I would sit with them and share tales of Max's antics – how he would steal socks from the laundry basket or beg for treats with those big, soulful eyes. These stories not only brought laughter amidst the tears but also reminded them of the joy and love Max had brought into our lives.

Emma, being the younger one, found solace in these stories. They allowed her to express her emotions freely, whether through giggles or sobs. Jack, on the other hand, often listened intently, nodding in recognition of the memories we shared.

As Max's condition deteriorated, I used these storytelling sessions to gently prepare them for what was to come. I wove in themes of love, loss, and the natural cycle of life, helping them understand that while our time with Max was finite, the bond we shared would never fade.

Helping Children Through Stories

Stories possess a unique power to help children process complex emotions and difficult situations. When facing pet loss, storytelling becomes an invaluable tool that allows children to explore their feelings through familiar narrative structures.

Creating stories about their pet's life celebrates the joy and adventures they shared together. Parents can guide children in crafting tales about their pet's favorite activities, silly moments, or special traditions. "Remember how Buster always chased his tail after breakfast?" or "What about the time Daisy discovered the garden sprinkler?" These personal narratives help preserve precious memories while providing emotional release.

Children often connect deeply with fictional characters who mirror their experiences. Books featuring characters dealing with pet loss show children they aren't alone in their grief. These stories normalize their emotions and provide examples of healthy coping mechanisms. Through characters' journeys, children witness different ways to honor their pet's memory and find comfort in shared experiences.

Interactive storytelling encourages children to express themselves creatively. They might draw pictures of their pet's adventures or write letters about their favorite memories. This creative outlet allows them to process grief at their own pace while maintaining a connection to their beloved companion.

Some families create ongoing narratives where their pet becomes a guardian angel or star in the sky, watching over them. While maintaining age-appropriate honesty about death, these gentle metaphors can provide comfort and help children develop their own understanding of loss and remembrance.

The key is ensuring these stories remain grounded in truth while providing emotional support. Rather than using stories to avoid reality, they should serve as bridges helping children navigate their grief journey. Through storytelling, children learn that their pet's story continues through their memories and the lasting impact of their love.

The Power of Visual Expression

Visual aids play a crucial role in processing grief, particularly when words fall short of capturing complex emotions. Illustrations, whether professionally created or personally drawn, provide a tangible way to express and understand feelings about pet loss.

The concept of the Rainbow Bridge has brought comfort to countless grieving pet owners. Artists have depicted this metaphorical bridge in various styles, from realistic pastoral scenes to abstract interpretations. These images often show peaceful meadows where beloved pets play freely, waiting to reunite with their human companions. While maintaining honest discussions about death, these illustrations can offer solace through their gentle symbolism.

Picture books dedicated to pet loss serve as valuable resources for all ages. Quality illustrations in these books capture subtle emotional nuances - the empty food bowl, the unused leash hanging by the door, or the indentation left on a favorite cushion. These visual cues validate the physical reminders of loss that survivors encounter daily.

Creating personal artwork can become a therapeutic practice. Simple sketches of your pet, even if not technically perfect, channel emotions into a concrete form. Consider starting a memory book with both photos and drawings, documenting special moments or characteristic behaviors that made your pet unique.

Children's picture books addressing pet loss deserve special consideration. Look for books with age-appropriate illustrations that balance realism with sensitivity. Effective visual narratives show characters moving through grief while honoring their pet's memory, demonstrating healthy coping mechanisms through accessible imagery.

Professional grief counselors often incorporate art therapy techniques, using guided drawing exercises to help process loss. These might include:

- Drawing your pet in their favorite place

- Creating a visual timeline of memorable moments

- Designing a memorial garden layout

- Illustrating the feelings associated with different memories

The combination of written and visual elements provides multiple pathways for understanding and expressing grief. Whether through published works or personal creation, visual representations offer another dimension to the healing journey.

Creative Expression for Children

Art and storytelling provide powerful outlets for children processing pet loss. These creative activities allow them to explore their emotions in a safe, constructive way while preserving precious memories of their companion.

Drawing offers immediate emotional release. Encourage children to illustrate their favorite moments with their pet - playing fetch in the backyard, snuggling during storytime, or sharing special treats. The act of drawing these scenes helps children focus on positive memories while working through their grief. Keep art supplies readily available and create a dedicated space where they can express themselves freely.

When children share their artwork, listen attentively to their explanations. Their descriptions often reveal deeper feelings about their loss. Some children might draw their pet in imagined scenarios - playing in heaven or watching over the family as an angel. These interpretations demonstrate how they're processing the concept of death and finding comfort in their own understanding.

Story writing allows children to maintain their connection with their pet through narrative. Suggest they write about their pet's adventures, either real or imagined. Some might choose to document their pet's life from the day they met to their final goodbye. Others might create fantasy tales where their pet embarks on magical journeys.

Consider these prompts to inspire their storytelling:

- "Write about your favorite day with [pet's name]"

- "Imagine where [pet's name] is now and what adventures they're having"

- "Tell the story of how [pet's name] came to live with us"

- "Write a letter to [pet's name] about your favorite memories together"

Provide blank books or journals where children can combine their stories and artwork. This creates a lasting tribute they can revisit whenever they miss their pet. Some children might want to share their creations with family members, while others may prefer to keep them private. Respect their choice while remaining available to discuss their work if they wish.

Through these creative exercises, children learn healthy ways to express grief while celebrating their pet's memory. Their artwork and stories become treasured keepsakes that honor the special bond they shared.

Creating Lasting Memorials

The process of remembering our pets can become a healing journey through intentional memorial activities. These tributes help transform raw grief into cherished memories while creating tangible connections to our departed companions.

Planting a memorial garden offers a living tribute that grows and changes with the seasons. Choose flowers that bloomed during your pet's lifetime or plants that mirror their personality - sturdy oak saplings for loyal guardians, graceful willows for gentle souls. As you tend to these growing memorials, the act of nurturing becomes a form of ongoing connection. Watch butterflies dance through your pet's garden, or birds nest in their memorial tree, bringing new life to spaces blessed by their memory.

Memory jars preserve precious moments in a uniquely personal way. Select a special container - perhaps one that matches your pet's favorite colors or reminds you of their spirit. Fill it with handwritten notes describing everyday moments: the way they greeted you after work, their favorite sunbathing spot, the sound of their purr or playful bark. Add small mementos like collar tags, beloved toys, or photos. On difficult days, reading these memories provides comfort and reminds us of the joy our pets brought to our lives.

Create a dedicated memorial space in your home or garden. This might include your pet's favorite bed adorned with fresh flowers, framed pawprints, or a collection of their most treasured possessions. These sacred spaces provide a focal point for remembrance and reflection, allowing us to maintain a spiritual connection with our departed friends.

Consider crafting personalized memorial stones or markers. Paint river rocks with your pet's name and special dates, or commission a custom garden marker featuring their likeness. These lasting tributes weather the elements while standing as permanent reminders of unconditional love.

Document your pet's story through a dedicated photo album or scrapbook. Include ticket stubs from shared adventures, holiday cards featuring their image, or notes from veterinary visits. These collections tell the complete story of your journey together, preserving both ordinary moments and milestone celebrations.

Your Pet's Memory Lives on Through Stories

Stories serve as powerful bridges between memory and healing, especially when helping children understand the lasting impact of their pet's life. Creating a family storybook dedicated to your pet offers a tangible way to preserve precious memories while teaching children about legacy and remembrance.

Begin by gathering family members to share their favorite memories. Each person brings unique perspectives and experiences - perhaps Mom remembers how the family cat always curled up on her laptop while she worked, while a child recalls teaching the dog new tricks in the backyard. These diverse viewpoints paint a fuller picture of your pet's personality and their role in the family.

Consider organizing your storybook chronologically, starting from the day your pet joined the family. Include milestone moments like birthdays, holidays, and special achievements. Photos enhance these memories - the first day home, vacation snapshots, or candid moments of everyday life. Children can contribute by decorating pages with drawings or adding their own written memories.

The process of creating this book opens natural conversations about your pet's impact. You might discover how your normally shy child gained confidence through training sessions, or how your pet helped the family cope during difficult times. These discussions highlight how pets shape our lives in profound ways.

Some families choose to include sections about:

- Funny habits or quirks that made their pet unique

- Times when their pet showed extraordinary loyalty or intelligence

- Ways their pet brought family members closer together

- Lessons learned through caring for their pet

This collaborative project helps children understand that while their pet is physically gone, their influence continues through shared stories and memories. The completed book becomes both a celebration of your pet's life and a tool for processing grief together.

As you work on the storybook, emphasize how these memories create a lasting legacy. Your pet's story becomes part of your family's history, passed down through generations. Children learn that love extends beyond physical presence and that sharing memories keeps their pet's spirit alive in meaningful ways.

Creating Meaningful Rituals for Closure

Rituals play an essential role in processing grief and finding closure after pet loss. For children especially, structured ceremonies provide tangible ways to say goodbye while honoring their pet's memory. These activities create sacred spaces where emotions can be expressed freely and memories celebrated openly.

A farewell ceremony doesn't need elaborate planning - its power lies in its personal meaning. Choose a peaceful outdoor setting like a favorite park or quiet corner of the backyard. Gather items that represent special memories: a cherished toy, collar, or favorite treat. Include photographs showing happy moments together.

Begin by forming a circle and lighting a memorial candle. The flame's gentle movement can help focus attention and create a calming atmosphere. Take turns sharing favorite memories or expressing gratitude for the joy your pet brought into your lives. Some families choose to read a poem or prayer, while others prefer moments of quiet reflection.

Children can participate by:

- Drawing pictures of their favorite memories

- Writing messages to their pet

- Singing a special song

- Releasing biodegradable balloons or floating flowers

- Planting seeds or bulbs in their pet's honor

Creating a regular ritual around remembrance provides ongoing comfort. Light a special candle during dinner once a week or month, using that time to share stories and acknowledge feelings. This practice shows children that while their pet is physically gone, their memory remains an important part of family life.

Some families establish annual traditions on their pet's birthday or adoption day:

- Making a donation to an animal shelter

- Volunteering at a rescue organization

- Creating new artwork for a memory wall

- Adding entries to a memory journal

- Sharing a meal featuring their pet's favorite people food

These rituals acknowledge the ongoing nature of grief while providing structured opportunities for expression and remembrance. They help children understand that it's okay to continue loving and missing their pet while moving forward in their healing journey.

Reflection

Creating a lasting tribute to your pet through storytelling provides a healthy outlet for grief while teaching valuable lessons about love, memory, and healing. Whether through formal storybooks, oral traditions, or creative projects, sharing these narratives helps both children and adults process their emotions and find meaning in their loss.

Stories validate the significant role pets play in our lives. They transform abstract concepts of death and remembrance into tangible experiences that children can grasp. Through storytelling, families discover that their pet's impact extends far beyond their physical presence - it lives on in the values they taught us, the joy they brought, and the bonds they helped forge.

The collaborative nature of memory-sharing strengthens family connections during difficult times. As each person contributes their unique perspective, a fuller picture emerges of how deeply intertwined our pets become in our daily lives. These shared experiences create a supportive environment where children feel safe expressing their feelings and asking questions about loss.

The process of documenting memories serves multiple purposes - it honors your pet's life, provides emotional release, and creates a lasting keepsake for future reflection. Children learn that it's possible to feel both sadness at their pet's absence and happiness when remembering good times. This understanding helps develop emotional resilience and healthy coping mechanisms.

By preserving your pet's story, you teach children that love transcends physical presence. The memories, lessons, and values your pet helped instill become part of your family's legacy, offering comfort and wisdom for years to come.

CHAPTER 13

DIY KEEPSAKES: CRAFTING MEMORY MEMENTOS

Losing Max was one of the hardest experiences our family has faced. Those big brown eyes and wagging tail had been constants in our lives for eight years. When the lymphoma diagnosis came, it felt like the world stopped spinning for a moment.

Emma was only nine at the time, her tiny hand patting Max's head as he lay motionless those final days. Jack, ever the pragmatist even at twelve years old, asked questions I didn't have answers for. How could I explain to them the cruelty of losing a best friend so soon?

In the weeks after Max was gone, the house felt eerily quiet. No more thumping tail against the kitchen floor or joyful barks greeting us at the door. We knew we needed to find a way to keep his spirit alive, so the kids and I began crafting memory mementos.

Emma carefully traced Max's paw print from an inkpad onto a small canvas, her brow furrowed in concentration. "This is so I'll never forget how big and strong he was," she explained, her small fingers gently shaping the print. Jack flipped through photos, curating a collage of Max's most hilarious and heart-melting moments caught on camera.

Creating Lasting Memories Through Personalized Keepsakes

The physical reminders of our pets hold profound meaning during the grieving process. While photographs capture moments frozen in time, personalized keepsakes offer tangible connections that we can hold, wear, or display to honor our beloved companions.

A pet's paw print preserved in clay or plaster creates a uniquely personal memorial. The distinct pattern of pads and tiny imperfections tell the story of countless walks, playful moments, and gentle touches shared between you and your pet. Many veterinary clinics offer paw print services during your pet's final visit, but you can also create these treasured molds at home using non-toxic modeling clay or plaster casting kits designed specifically for this purpose.

Custom jewelry transforms your pet's memory into wearable art that keeps them close to your heart. Consider pendants engraved with their name or initials, charm bracelets featuring their breed or species, or lockets that hold a small photo or lock of fur. Some artisans even specialize in creating unique pieces that incorporate your pet's actual paw print or nose print into the design.

These keepsakes serve as more than mere decorative items - they become touchstones during difficult moments, offering comfort when grief feels overwhelming. Running your fingers across a paw print or touching a necklace bearing your pet's name can ground you in memories of their love and presence.

The process of creating these mementos also provides an opportunity for mindful reflection. As you work with materials or collaborate with artisans to design the perfect piece, you engage in an act of intentional remembrance. This creative expression of grief helps channel emotions into something beautiful and lasting.

Consider displaying these keepsakes in spaces where you spend time daily. A paw print casting might find its home on your desk, while a piece of memorial jewelry becomes part of your daily routine. These visible reminders help integrate your pet's memory into your ongoing life story, acknowledging both their absence and their lasting impact on your heart.

Creating Personal Memorials Through DIY Projects

The process of creating handmade memorials offers therapeutic benefits while producing cherished keepsakes. Let's explore two meaningful projects you can create at home to honor your pet's memory.

Memory Box Creation:

1. Select a sturdy wooden or decorative box that reflects your pet's personality. Consider size carefully - ensure it accommodates collars, toys, and other mementos.

2. Sand the surface if using unfinished wood, then apply paint or stain in colors that remind you of your pet.

3. Line the interior with soft fabric like velvet or felt to protect delicate items.

4. Create compartments using small dividers or jewelry box inserts to organize different types of memories.

5. Decorate the exterior with photos, paw prints, or meaningful quotes using decoupage techniques.

6. Add personal touches like your pet's name or dates using stencils or letter transfers.

Memory Quilt or Pillow:

1. Gather your pet's favorite blankets, beds, or clothing items. Include any fabric that holds special meaning.

2. Wash all materials thoroughly and iron them flat for easier handling.

3. Cut fabric into uniform squares or shapes that work with your design vision.

4. Arrange pieces in a pattern that tells your pet's story - perhaps chrono-

logically or by theme.

5. If working with delicate materials, back them with interfacing for stability.

6. Sew pieces together by hand or machine, taking time to remember the associated memories.

7. Add batting and backing for quilts, or stuffing for pillows.

8. Consider incorporating photos printed on fabric or embroidered details like your pet's name.

For both projects, set aside dedicated time in a quiet space where you can work undisturbed. Keep tissues nearby - tears are natural and healing as you handle items that spark memories. Take breaks when needed, and remember there's no rush to complete these projects. The creation process itself offers valuable time for reflection and emotional processing.

Incorporating Cherished Items into Memorial Crafts

Personal items that belonged to your pet hold deep emotional significance and can become powerful elements in memorial projects. The familiar jingle of tags or the worn texture of a favorite collar can transport us back to precious moments shared with our companions.

Consider transforming your pet's collar into a wrapped bracelet or hanging decoration. The metal tags can be incorporated into wind chimes, creating gentle music that reminds you of their presence. Some pet parents choose to have tags engraved with special dates or messages before incorporating them into jewelry or display pieces.

Photos capture unique personalities and special moments. Select images that showcase your pet's character - perhaps that endearing head tilt, or the way they sprawled in their favorite sunspot. These can be transferred onto various surfaces using mod podge or special photo transfer mediums. Create a photo wall collage, or incorporate prints into decorative boxes and frames.

Original artwork adds another layer of meaning to memorial pieces. Commission an artist to create a portrait based on your favorite photo, or paint one yourself if you're artistically inclined. Even simple sketches can capture essential characteristics - the curve of a tail, the shape of ears, or that special look in their eyes.

Consider preserving fur clippings in clear ornaments or incorporating them into felted wool projects. Some crafters create small cloth sachets filled with fur to keep close. These tactile reminders can provide comfort during difficult moments.

For those who have paw print impressions, these unique marks can be cast in clay, carved into wood, or transferred onto fabric. Each print tells a story of your pet's physical presence and the paths you walked together.

When selecting materials, focus on items that spark joy rather than sadness. Choose objects that remind you of happy moments and celebrations of your pet's life rather than their final days.

Therapeutic Value of Crafting

The act of creating memorial pieces offers more than just tangible keepsakes - it provides a therapeutic pathway through grief. When your hands are busy crafting, your mind enters a state of focused meditation. This natural flow state allows emotions to process while channeling energy into something meaningful and beautiful.

Working with materials connected to your pet creates space for positive memories to surface. As you handle a beloved collar or sort through photographs, each item sparks recollections of joyful moments. The repetitive motions of crafting - whether stringing beads, weaving fabric, or molding clay - create a rhythm that helps steady racing thoughts and calm anxious energy.

Crafting in the company of family members adds another layer of healing. Children especially benefit from hands-on projects that help them express complex emotions. A family crafting session opens natural opportunities for sharing stories and memories. As you work side by side, conversations flow more easily. Tears and laughter intermingle as you recall funny moments or special quirks.

Consider setting up a dedicated crafting space where family members can drop in when they feel ready. Stock it with basic supplies and photos. This creates an inviting environment for spontaneous creativity and connection. Some families choose to craft memorial pieces during significant dates like adoption anniversaries or birthdays, making the creative process part of their ongoing remembrance rituals.

The finished pieces serve as touchstones for healing, but the act of creating them is equally valuable. Each step - from gathering materials to completing final details - provides opportunities to honor your pet's memory while moving forward through grief. The process teaches us that beauty can emerge from loss, and that our love for our pets continues to inspire creativity and connection.

Reflection

The healing power of creative expression remains one of our most potent tools for processing grief. Through crafting memorial pieces, we transform our pain into beauty while keeping our pet's memory alive in tangible ways. These physical reminders serve not just as decorative items, but as bridges between past and present - allowing us to maintain meaningful connections even as we move forward.

Whether working alone or alongside family members, the act of creating provides a gentle pathway through difficult emotions. The focused attention required for crafting offers respite from overwhelming feelings while still honoring our need to remember and reflect. Each piece we create tells a story - of love, of loss, of the unique bond we shared with our pet.

The therapeutic benefits extend beyond the finished product. The process itself teaches valuable lessons about healing - that it takes time, that it doesn't need to be perfect, that beauty can emerge from grief when we allow ourselves to explore it creatively. As we work with our hands, we discover new ways to hold our memories close while gradually accepting change.

Most importantly, creative memorial projects remind us that our love for our pets continues to inspire and move us forward. Their presence in our lives sparked joy and connection - qualities that live on through the pieces we craft in their honor. While the pain of loss may linger, channeling it into creative expression helps transform grief into lasting tributes that comfort and heal.

CHAPTER 14

CREATING A MEMORY GARDEN: A LIVING TRIBUTE

The loss of Max hit our family hard. That goofy, loving golden retriever had been by our side for eight wonderful years, and his absence left an unmistakable void. In the depths of our grief, we struggled to find solace - until we had the idea to create a memory garden in Max's honor.

Working together in the backyard, we prepared a small patch of soil where vibrant flowers would soon bloom. Each member of the family carefully selected seeds and bulbs representative of Max's sunny spirit. My son chose sunflowers, their bright petals reminiscent of Max's ever-wagging tail. My daughter opted for daffodils, cheerful harbingers of spring just like Max greeted each new day.

As we planted those seeds, we shared stories and laughed through tears, reminiscing about Max's antics - how he'd joyfully roll in the grass, kick up dirt, then bound inside leaving muddy pawprints across the kitchen floor. With each handful of soil patted into place, we infused the garden with memories of his boundless energy and affection.

Creating a Living Memorial

The ancient practice of memorial gardens dates back thousands of years, offering a profound way to honor those we've lost while nurturing new life. For pet owners, creating a dedicated space filled with carefully chosen plants provides both a therapeutic outlet and a lasting tribute to their beloved companion.

A memory garden transforms grief into growth, converting an empty space into a sanctuary of remembrance. The process begins with selecting the perfect location - perhaps that sunny corner where your cat loved to bask, or near the window where your dog spent hours watching the world go by. These meaningful spots hold echoes of precious moments, making them ideal foundations for a living memorial.

The selection of plants adds layers of symbolism to your garden. Forget-me-nots, with their delicate blue blooms, speak directly to remembrance. Rosemary, long associated with memory, releases its aromatic oils with each gentle touch. For pets who loved to chase butterflies, butterfly bushes attract these winged visitors while adding splashes of purple and pink. White roses represent purity and innocence, while sturdy evergreens stand as symbols of enduring love.

Consider incorporating elements that reflected your pet's personality. A climbing vine might honor an adventurous spirit, while low-growing ground covers could commemorate a pet who loved to burrow. Catnip or pet grass can acknowledge their favorite treats, creating a space that truly captures their essence.

The physical act of gardening - digging in the soil, planting seedlings, pulling weeds - provides a meditative outlet for grief. Each season brings new growth and changes, mirroring the journey through loss while maintaining a connection to your pet's memory. The garden becomes a living, breathing space that evolves and flourishes, just as your memories remain vibrant and alive.

This special place offers more than just visual beauty. It becomes a destination for reflection, a quiet corner where you can feel close to your pet while surrounded by nature's gentle reminders of life's continuous cycle. As plants take root and bloom, they create a lasting tribute that honors your pet's memory through every changing season.

Planning and Planting

When planning your memory garden, start with a simple sketch that maps out different areas and plant heights. Consider your climate zone and seasonal changes to ensure your chosen plants will thrive year-round. Local nurseries can guide you toward native species that require minimal maintenance while providing continuous blooms.

If your pet had favorite outdoor spots, incorporate similar plants into your design. Did they love rolling in patches of grass? Create a small lawn area with soft ornamental grasses. Were they drawn to certain flowers? Plant clusters of these blooms as focal points. For cats who enjoyed watching birds, include berry-producing shrubs that attract feathered visitors.

Layer your plantings to create visual interest throughout the seasons. Place taller plants like ornamental grasses or small flowering trees toward the back, medium-height perennials in the middle, and ground covers or creeping plants in front. This creates natural depth while ensuring all elements remain visible.

A commemorative stone or plaque forms the heart of your memorial garden. Choose weather-resistant materials like granite or cast bronze that will withstand the elements. Consider engraving your pet's name, special dates, or a meaningful quote. Position this marker where it catches natural light or creates a focal point among the plantings.

Integrate practical elements that make tending the garden easier. Install stepping stones for access during wet weather. Add mulch to retain moisture and reduce weeding. Consider a small bench or seating area where you can sit and reflect.

For year-round interest, mix evergreen plants with seasonal bloomers. Spring bulbs like daffodils and tulips herald new beginnings. Summer perennials provide continuous color. Fall-blooming asters and chrysanthemums extend the growing season. Even in winter, ornamental grasses and evergreens maintain the garden's structure.

Water features add another sensory dimension. A small fountain or birdbath creates soothing sounds while attracting wildlife. If your pet loved playing with running water, consider a cascading feature that captures that playful spirit.

Remember to include space for future additions. As your garden grows, you might want to add new plants that remind you of special memories or incorporate decorative elements like wind chimes or solar lights.

Add Personal Elements

A memory garden becomes more meaningful when you incorporate elements that reflect your pet's unique personality and the special bond you shared. Consider how your pet's character can guide your design choices. For a playful dog who loved to dig, create dedicated digging areas filled with pet-safe plants. For a cat who enjoyed sunbathing, design sunny spots with flat rocks or raised platforms.

Plant selection offers endless possibilities for personalization. A majestic oak or flowering dogwood serves as a living tribute that grows stronger each year. Choose a species that matches your pet's traits - perhaps a sturdy maple for a loyal companion, or a graceful weeping cherry for a gentle soul. As these trees mature, they become lasting monuments to your pet's memory.

Create pathways through your garden using personalized stepping stones. Each stone can hold a different memory - the day you met, favorite activities, or special nicknames. Use weather-resistant paint or have them professionally engraved. Arrange them to form a meandering path that encourages contemplation as you walk through your garden.

Consider incorporating items that belonged to your pet. A weathered collar can become a unique garden ornament, or their favorite toy might inspire a decorative element. Transform their water bowl into a small planter for succulents or convert their bed into a raised flower bed filled with their favorite colors.

Add personal touches that capture specific memories. If your pet loved chasing butterflies, plant butterfly-attracting flowers like lantana or butterfly bush. For those afternoon naps in the sun, create a dedicated seating area where you can sit and remember those peaceful moments.

Remember that your memory garden will evolve over time, just as your grief journey progresses. Start small with a few meaningful elements and allow the space to grow organically. Each new addition becomes part of your healing process, creating a living tribute that honors your beloved companion's legacy.

Role of Memory Garden in Healing

A memory garden offers more than just a beautiful space - it provides an ongoing connection to your pet through the ritual of gardening itself. Each visit becomes a chance to nurture both the plants and your healing process. The simple act of pulling weeds, pruning branches, or watering flowers creates quiet moments for reflection and remembrance.

Make these garden visits part of your regular routine. Perhaps start each morning by deadheading spent blooms while enjoying your coffee, or end your day watching the sunset from a garden bench. These consistent rituals help ground you in the present while honoring your pet's memory.

The changing seasons in your garden mirror the natural cycles of grief and renewal. Spring brings fresh growth and new beginnings as bulbs push through the soil. Summer's abundant blooms celebrate the joy your pet brought to your life. Fall's changing colors remind us that transformation is natural. Even winter's dormant period offers time for quiet contemplation.

Use seasonal plantings to mark significant dates in your pet's life. Plant spring bulbs that will bloom around their birthday or choose fall mums to flower near the anniversary of their passing. These natural timekeepers help transform difficult dates into opportunities for meaningful remembrance.

The physical work of gardening - digging in the soil, pruning branches, spreading mulch - provides a healthy outlet for grief's physical manifestations.

The repetitive motions can be meditative, allowing emotions to flow naturally while your hands stay busy with purposeful tasks.

Weather and seasonal changes may affect how often you can work in the garden, but even viewing it through a window on rainy days can provide comfort. The garden's constant presence, even during dormant periods, reminds us that growth and healing continue beneath the surface.

As your garden matures, you'll find that tending to it becomes less about active grief and more about peaceful remembrance. New plants and features can be added as you feel ready, allowing the space to evolve along with your healing journey.

Reflection

A memory garden transforms grief into growth through the simple yet profound act of nurturing life. Like the perennial flowers that return each spring, our memories of beloved pets remain eternally rooted in our hearts. The garden provides both a sacred space for remembrance and an active pathway toward healing.

Through seasonal changes and cycles of growth, these living memorials remind us that grief evolves naturally over time. Just as gardens require patience, care, and attention, so too does our journey through loss. Each bloom, each new leaf, each moment spent tending the space becomes part of an ongoing dialogue with our memories.

The physical connection to the earth grounds us in the present while honoring the past. Whether sitting quietly among the flowers or actively working the soil, the garden offers countless opportunities for meditation, reflection, and peace. It stands as a testament to love that continues to grow and flourish, even after loss.

As time passes, the garden becomes less a monument to grief and more a celebration of the joy and companionship our pets brought to our lives. In this way, memory gardens help transform our pain into something beautiful -

a living, breathing tribute that continues to bring comfort and meaning to our lives.

CHAPTER 15

PERSONALIZED CEREMONIES: DESIGNING FAREWELL RITUALS

When Max's lymphoma became too advanced to treat, we made the agonizing decision to have him put to sleep. Those final moments were some of the most heartbreaking of my life. As I stroked his golden fur and he drifted off peacefully, I promised Max I would honor his memory.

In the days after, my family came together to design rituals to say goodbye. We planted a cherry tree sapling in the backyard, Max's favorite spot for sunbathing. Each person added a fistful of soil from the hole, creating a living connection. We placed his worn toy bunny and a tuft of his fur in a small wooden box to bury beneath the tree's roots. At the trunk, we installed a carved plaque with his name and "Forever Loved." Watering the sapling became a family ritual each morning as we reflected on Max's unconditional love and loyalty.

Creating Meaningful Farewell Ceremonies

Saying goodbye to a beloved pet deserves the same reverence and care as any significant life transition. A thoughtfully planned farewell ceremony provides crucial closure while celebrating the profound bond you shared with your companion.

Candlelight ceremonies offer an intimate setting for remembrance. Gather loved ones in a circle, each holding a candle representing your pet's light in your lives. As each person lights their candle, they can share a cherished memory or express what made your pet special. The warm glow creates a peaceful atmosphere for collective grieving and healing.

Some families choose to release biodegradable sky lanterns at dusk. Each family member writes a personal message or draws a picture on their lantern before releasing it into the evening sky. The gentle ascent of the illuminated lanterns symbolizes letting go while maintaining connection through memory. For those concerned about environmental impact, consider alternatives like planting wildflower seeds or releasing bubbles.

Beach ceremonies allow for natural elements to play a role in your farewell. Write messages in the sand, build a temporary memorial with shells and stones, or scatter pet-safe flower petals into the waves. The ocean's constant motion reminds us that grief ebbs and flows, while the vastness of the horizon offers perspective on life's continuous journey.

For those seeking a more structured approach, creating a memorial service similar to traditional funerals can provide familiar comfort. Include readings of pet-themed poetry, display photo collections, or play music that reminds you of happy moments together. Share stories that capture your pet's unique personality and the joy they brought to your life.

Consider incorporating elements that were meaningful to your pet - perhaps scattering treats in their favorite park, hanging wind chimes in their sunbathing spot, or placing their favorite toy in a special memory box. These personal touches make the ceremony uniquely meaningful to your shared experiences.

Planning a Ceremony

Planning a meaningful farewell ceremony requires thoughtful consideration of elements that honor your pet's unique life and personality. The location choice sets the foundation for the entire experience. Consider spaces that held special meaning - perhaps the backyard where they chased butterflies, their favorite hiking trail, or the park where they made furry friends.

Indoor venues offer privacy and weather protection. Transform your living room into a memorial space by arranging photos, toys, and mementos. Community pet crematoriums often provide dedicated rooms for ceremonies, equipped with comfortable seating and audio-visual capabilities for sharing photo slideshows.

Writing a eulogy helps articulate your feelings while celebrating your pet's life story. Begin by reflecting on their arrival into your life - the circumstances of their adoption or birth, their distinctive personality traits, and the joy they brought to everyday moments. Include specific memories that showcase their character: the way they greeted you after work, their unusual habits, or their interactions with family members.

Structure your eulogy chronologically or thematically. You might focus on their roles - loyal protector, gentle companion, or mischievous entertainer. Share how they supported you through life changes or taught valuable lessons about love and presence. Include humorous anecdotes to balance the emotional weight and celebrate their spirit.

Record stories from each person in your family. These preserved memories become precious keepsakes, offering comfort during difficult moments and ensuring your pet's legacy lives on through the stories that touched so many hearts.

Incorporating Cultural Elements

Cultural and spiritual elements can provide profound comfort during pet loss ceremonies, offering frameworks for understanding and processing grief. Many belief systems acknowledge the spiritual significance of animals and their connection to humans, providing rich traditions to draw from when planning a memorial.

Buddhist traditions emphasize impermanence and compassion, offering practices like meditation or chanting that can bring peace during the ceremony. Consider incorporating a moment of mindful silence to honor your pet's presence in your life, or lighting incense as a symbol of transformation and purification.

Native American customs often recognize animals as spiritual teachers and guides. Creating a sacred circle with natural elements like stones, feathers, or shells can represent the cyclical nature of life and death. Smudging ceremonies using sage or sweetgrass can cleanse the space and participants' spirits.

Christian services might include readings about God's care for all creatures or prayers of thanksgiving for the gift of animal companionship. Psalms speaking of creation and divine love resonate deeply during pet memorials. Some churches even offer pet blessing services or special remembrance masses.

For those following earth-based spiritualities, creating an altar with meaningful objects honors your pet's memory. Place their collar, favorite toy, or photos alongside symbols of the elements - a candle for fire, water in a bowl, earth in a small dish, and feathers for air. This sacred space becomes a focal point for reflection and remembrance.

Jewish traditions value the concept of "tzaar baalei chayim" - preventing animal suffering - and recognize the importance of treating animals with kindness. While formal pet funerals aren't traditional, incorporating elements like readings from Jewish texts about compassion toward animals can be meaningful.

For those who don't follow specific religious traditions, creating personalized rituals can be equally powerful. Consider writing and reading a blessing that captures your unique relationship with your pet. Light candles representing different aspects of their personality or stages of your journey together. Use symbols that hold personal significance - perhaps a shell from a beach they loved or leaves from their favorite walking path.

Remember that combining elements from different traditions or creating entirely new ones is perfectly acceptable. The key is choosing practices that resonate with your beliefs and honor your pet's memory in ways that feel authentic and meaningful to you.

Reflection

Ceremonies and rituals serve as powerful tools for processing grief and finding closure after the loss of a beloved pet. Through thoughtfully planned farewells, we create sacred spaces to honor our companions and begin the healing journey.

The act of gathering with others who understand our loss provides validation and support during this challenging transition. These moments of remembrance help anchor our memories and give shape to our grief.

Recording these ceremonies preserves not just the event itself, but captures the love and support shown by friends and family. These documented moments become treasured keepsakes, offering comfort during difficult times and allowing us to revisit the outpouring of compassion shown during our time of loss.

The flexibility to personalize these rituals ensures they remain meaningful and authentic to both our pet's memory and our own needs. While ceremonies mark important milestones in our grief journey, they represent stepping stones rather than endpoints. They provide structure and meaning during a time of chaos, helping us navigate the complex emotions of loss while honoring the profound impact our pets had on our lives.

Through these intentional acts of remembrance, we create lasting tributes that acknowledge both our loss and the enduring love we hold for our departed companions. These ceremonies become cornerstones in our healing process, offering comfort and connection as we move forward while keeping our pet's memory alive in our hearts.

CHAPTER 16

UNDERSTANDING READINESS: IS IT TIME FOR ANOTHER PET?

The decision to welcome another pet into our lives was not an easy one. As I sat on the back porch, gazing out at Max's favorite sunny spot in the yard, a wave of memories washed over me. I could almost see his golden form basking in the warmth, his tail thumping contentedly against the worn wooden planks.

How could we even consider bringing another furry companion into our home when the ache of Max's absence still felt so raw? His battle with lymphoma had been merciless, and the guilt of that final, gut-wrenching choice to end his suffering lingered like a heavy fog.

Yet, as I reminisced about the boundless joy Max had brought into our lives, a glimmer of hope began to flicker. The house felt so empty without his cheerful greetings and the pitter-patter of his paws trailing behind us. Could opening our hearts to a new pet help fill the void left by his passing?

Considering a New Pet - Are You Ready?

The decision to welcome a new pet into your life after loss carries profound emotional weight. This choice deserves careful consideration, as premature adoption can complicate your healing journey while waiting too long might deprive you of the joy and companionship you're ready to embrace.

Your heart often signals readiness through subtle shifts in perspective. When thoughts of a new pet spark genuine excitement rather than guilt or obligation, it suggests emotional healing has progressed. Pay attention to how you react when seeing other people's pets - if you find yourself smiling instead of crying, your grief may be transforming into acceptance.

Consider your motivations carefully. Are you seeking to fill an emptiness, or do you feel genuinely open to building a new relationship? The distinction matters. A healthy desire for pet companionship stems from having processed your loss while maintaining cherished memories of your previous pet. Rushing into adoption to escape grief often leads to complicated emotions and unfair expectations for the new animal.

Family dynamics play a crucial role in this decision. Each family member may process grief differently and reach readiness at varying times. Open discussions about everyone's feelings help ensure the timing feels right for all involved. Children particularly need space to express their thoughts about welcoming a new pet.

Take inventory of practical factors alongside emotional ones. Consider your current lifestyle, schedule, and resources. Readiness involves both heart and logistics - having the emotional capacity to bond while being able to meet a new pet's needs.

Remember that readiness doesn't mean forgetting. You can honor your deceased pet's memory while opening your heart to new love. Many find that previous pet relationships enhance their capacity for future bonds rather than diminishing them.

Trust your instincts but remain honest with yourself. If uncertainty persists, there's no harm in waiting. The right timing allows you to fully embrace the joy of new pet companionship without emotional reservation.

Self-Reflection Questions to Consider

Before making the decision to adopt a new pet, take time to explore your emotional landscape through these thoughtful questions. Write your answers in a journal, allowing yourself to respond honestly without judgment.

Consider your current emotional state:

- When you look at photos of your deceased pet, what emotions arise first?

- How do you feel when friends or family mention getting a new pet?

- Are you able to share happy memories of your pet without becoming overwhelmed?

- Do you still experience frequent crying spells when thinking about your loss?

Examine your motivations:

- What draws you to the idea of adopting another pet?

- Are you seeking to recreate the relationship you had with your previous pet?

- Would you feel guilty giving attention and love to a new animal?

- Have you fully processed your grief, or are you trying to escape it?

Assess practical readiness:

- Can you provide the time and energy a new pet requires?

- Are you financially prepared for routine and emergency veterinary care?

- Does your living situation accommodate pet ownership?

- Have you researched the specific needs of the type of pet you're considering?

Evaluate family dynamics:

- How do other household members feel about getting a new pet?

- Have children in the family expressed their thoughts about adoption?

- Is everyone willing to share in pet care responsibilities?

- Has the family reached consensus about timing?

These questions serve as guideposts rather than a definitive checklist. Your answers may change over time, and that's perfectly normal. Revisit them periodically to track your emotional progress and readiness for this significant step.

Importance of Timing

The decision to welcome a new pet into your life after loss carries profound emotional weight, and timing plays a crucial role in this deeply personal choice. While some individuals feel ready to open their hearts to a new companion within weeks, others may need months or even years to process their grief. Neither timeline is wrong - each person's journey through loss follows its own unique path.

Society often pressures grieving pet owners with well-meaning but misguided advice about "getting over it" by adopting another pet quickly. These external pressures can create unnecessary stress during an already difficult period. Your readiness to adopt depends on numerous factors beyond just the passage of time.

Consider your current life circumstances. Are you in the midst of other major changes - moving homes, switching jobs, or dealing with family obligations? Adding a new pet during periods of transition may create additional stress for both you and the animal. A stable environment allows you to focus on building a strong foundation with your new companion.

Your emotional capacity also influences timing. If you find yourself still breaking down at the sight of your previous pet's belongings or unable to discuss them without intense pain, you may need more time to process these feelings. There's no shame in waiting until you can think of your deceased pet with more peace than anguish.

Financial readiness represents another key timing consideration. Pet ownership involves ongoing costs for food, supplies, and veterinary care. Ensure you have the resources to provide properly for a new animal before making this commitment.

Your living situation may also impact timing. Rental agreements, space constraints, and the presence of other pets or family members all factor into this decision. Take time to evaluate whether your current circumstances can accommodate the specific needs of the type of pet you're considering.

Remember that readiness isn't linear. You might feel prepared one day and overwhelmed the next. This fluctuation is normal and doesn't indicate failure or regression in your grief journey. Trust your instincts and give yourself permission to wait until the timing feels consistently right.

Patience When Making a Decision

The journey of deciding when to welcome a new pet requires immense self-compassion and patience. Many pet owners struggle with feelings of guilt or betrayal when considering another animal companion, viewing it as somehow dishonoring their deceased pet's memory. These emotions, while natural, shouldn't be rushed away or dismissed.

Give yourself permission to sit with uncertainty. Some days you might feel ready to visit shelters and browse adoption websites. Other days, the mere thought of another pet might trigger fresh waves of grief. Both reactions are valid parts of the healing process.

Rather than viewing these mixed feelings as setbacks, recognize them as signs that you're processing your loss thoughtfully and honestly. There's no prize for moving through grief quickly, and no penalty for taking extra time to ensure you're emotionally prepared.

Trusted friends and family members can provide valuable perspective during this decision-making period. Share your concerns with those who understood your bond with your previous pet. They may offer insights you haven't considered or simply provide a compassionate ear as you work through your feelings.

However, remember that while others can provide support and guidance, they can't determine your readiness for you. Only you can truly gauge when your heart has healed enough to forge a new bond. Trust your instincts and resist pressure - whether external or self-imposed - to move faster than feels comfortable.

If you find yourself consistently questioning whether you're ready, that hesitation itself might be your answer. Taking additional time to process your grief won't diminish your capacity to love another pet in the future. Instead, it ensures that when you do choose to adopt, you can do so from a place of emotional strength and clarity.

Reflection

The decision to welcome a new pet marks a deeply personal milestone in the grief journey. This chapter explored the complex emotions and considerations involved in determining readiness for another animal companion. We discussed the importance of self-reflection, patience, and trusting one's emotional compass when contemplating this significant step.

Remember that healing from pet loss follows no predetermined timeline. Your journey belongs to you alone, and the choice to adopt again should arise from a place of emotional preparedness rather than external expectations. By taking time to process your grief fully, you honor both your departed pet's memory and your future capacity to forge meaningful bonds with new animal companions.

The questions and guidance provided in this chapter serve as tools for self-discovery, not rigid benchmarks. Use them to check in with yourself periodically, always remembering that uncertainty or hesitation signals healthy emotional awareness rather than weakness.

As you continue to navigate this aspect of your grief journey, maintain compassion for yourself. Your willingness to carefully consider the timing of welcoming a new pet demonstrates respect for both your emotional needs and the responsibility of pet guardianship. Trust that when the time feels right, you'll recognize it with clarity and conviction.

CHAPTER 17

THE CYCLE OF LOVE AND LOSS: EMBRACING NEW RELATIONSHIPS

The weeks after Max's passing felt like an endless fog of sorrow. His golden fur no longer tumbled across the living room floor, his tail didn't thump happily against the couch when I came home. The house felt painfully quiet without his welcoming barks. During those early days of grief, the idea of opening my heart to another furry companion seemed unfathomable. How could I even consider replacing the dog who had been by my side for the last eight years?

But as the months went on and the rawness of grief softened into bittersweet memories, I began to feel glimmers of readiness. Max's love had been one of the greatest gifts of my life - a bond that transcended language and species. Perhaps by honoring his spirit through giving that gift to another animal in need, I could begin embracing the possibility of new relationships and experiences awaiting me.

The Circle of Love and Loss

The journey of pet companionship weaves an intricate pattern of joy and sorrow, each thread essential to the tapestry of our lives. As we navigate the path of healing from pet loss, understanding this cyclical nature helps us find meaning in both the love we've shared and the grief we experience.

Every pet owner embarks on this journey knowing, somewhere in their heart, that their time together will be limited. Yet we choose to open our hearts again and again because the profound joy of sharing our lives with animal companions far outweighs the inevitable pain of saying goodbye.

This cycle begins the moment we first lock eyes with a potential new friend at a shelter, or hold a tiny puppy or kitten in our arms. In those precious early moments, we make an unspoken pact - to cherish every moment while accepting that our time together is finite.

The daily rhythms of pet ownership - the morning greetings, shared meals, walks, and quiet moments of connection - create a symphony of experiences that enrich our lives immeasurably. These moments accumulate into years of unconditional love, teaching us lessons about presence, joy, and living in the moment.

When loss comes, it can feel like the music has stopped. The silence of their absence echoes through our homes and hearts. Yet even in this profound grief, we carry forward the gifts our pets gave us - the capacity to love deeply, to find joy in simple moments, and to open ourselves to connection despite knowing it cannot last forever.

This understanding of life's circular nature doesn't diminish our grief, but it can help us contextualize it as part of a greater whole. Just as seasons change and stars complete their cycles in the night sky, the journey of pet companionship follows its own natural rhythm of beginnings and endings, each cycle leaving us forever changed.

The love we share with our pets transforms us, expanding our capacity for compassion and deepening our understanding of life's precious impermanence.

Each pet that touches our lives adds to this wisdom, creating layers of experience that shape who we become.

Emotional Benefits of New Relationships

While the loss of a beloved pet creates a void that can never be exactly filled, opening our hearts to new animal companions offers unique opportunities for healing and growth. Each new relationship brings its own special dynamic, helping us rediscover the transformative power of the human-animal bond.

When we welcome a new pet into our lives, we experience afresh the profound gift of unconditional love. Animals have an extraordinary capacity to accept us exactly as we are, offering comfort without judgment or expectation. This pure acceptance can be especially healing for those still carrying grief, as it reminds us that our capacity to give and receive love remains intact.

The daily routines of caring for a new pet help restore structure and purpose to our lives. Morning walks, feeding times, and play sessions create anchoring points throughout the day. These activities gradually shift our focus from loss toward the present moment, where joy can begin to flourish again.

New pets also have a remarkable ability to help us laugh and smile, even when we thought we couldn't. Their playful antics, unique personalities, and earnest attempts to understand our world can bring unexpected moments of delight. These glimpses of happiness don't dishonor our previous pet's memory - rather, they honor the lessons of love and joy our former companions taught us.

The process of bonding with a new pet allows us to exercise our emotional muscles in healthy ways. We learn to balance honoring our past relationships while remaining open to new connections. This emotional flexibility strengthens our resilience and deepens our understanding of love's endless capacity to grow and evolve.

Creating new routines and rituals with a new pet helps establish fresh patterns of companionship while respecting the unique memories of our previous relationship. Each walk becomes an opportunity to both remember and move forward, each shared moment a chance to heal while building something new.

Through these new bonds, we often discover that our hearts have an infinite capacity for love. Rather than replacing our previous pet, new companions add their own distinct chapters to our ongoing story of pet guardianship.

Fears of Re-Experiencing Loss

The prospect of loving and potentially losing another pet can feel overwhelming. Many people find themselves hesitating to form new bonds, haunted by the pain of their previous loss. This fear, while completely natural, can prevent us from experiencing the profound joy and healing that new animal relationships offer.

Understanding and acknowledging these fears is the first step toward managing them. The anxiety about future loss often stems from our deep capacity for love - we know how intensely we can bond with our pets, which makes the thought of another goodbye seem unbearable. However, this same depth of feeling also enables us to create meaningful new connections.

Rather than letting fear dictate our choices, we can learn to focus on the present moments with a new pet. Each day brings opportunities for joy, connection, and growth. By practicing mindfulness during daily activities like feeding, grooming, or playing, we anchor ourselves in the now rather than projecting into a feared future.

Our previous experiences with pet loss, though painful, have equipped us with valuable coping skills and emotional resilience. We've learned how to navigate grief, discovered support systems, and developed personal strategies for healing. This knowledge doesn't make future losses easier, but it provides us with tools and confidence in our ability to survive difficult emotions.

Building resilience means acknowledging that love always carries risk. Yet the richness and meaning our pets bring to our lives far outweigh the pain of eventual separation. Each relationship teaches us more about ourselves and expands our capacity for compassion and connection.

Remember that choosing to love again despite past hurt is an act of courage. It demonstrates trust in our ability to heal and grow through challenging experiences. While we can't control how long our pets will be with us, we can control how fully we embrace the time we have together.

Through mindful presence and the wisdom gained from past experiences, we can learn to balance awareness of life's impermanence with wholehearted engagement in current relationships. This balance allows us to honor both our fears and our desire for connection, creating space for new bonds to flourish.

Embrace Vulnerability

Opening ourselves to new pet relationships requires embracing vulnerability. While our instinct might be to protect ourselves from future pain, this defensive stance can prevent us from experiencing the profound healing and joy that comes from forming new bonds.

Consider visiting local animal shelters or rescue organizations. Each animal there has its own story of loss and resilience. Their ability to trust and love again, despite past hardships, can inspire our own journey toward healing. Many shelter volunteers and staff members have experienced pet loss themselves and understand the complex emotions involved in adopting again.

Support groups and online communities offer countless stories of people who have successfully navigated the path from grief to new relationships. These testimonials remind us that forming new bonds doesn't diminish our love for pets we've lost. Instead, each relationship adds another layer to our capacity for compassion and understanding.

Connecting with others who have walked this path provides practical insights and emotional validation. They can share strategies for managing anxiety about potential future loss while fully embracing the present moment with a new pet. Their experiences demonstrate that choosing to love again isn't about replacing what was lost, but about creating space for new connections.

The journey toward new pet relationships often progresses in small steps. Some people start by fostering animals, providing temporary homes while working through their feelings about permanent adoption. Others volunteer at shelters or pet-sit for friends, gradually rebuilding their confidence in forming attachments.

Remember that vulnerability isn't weakness - it's courage in action. By opening ourselves to new possibilities, we honor both our past pets and our own capacity for growth and healing.

Reflection

The journey through pet loss and healing culminates in the profound understanding that vulnerability serves as a gateway to deeper connections. While the path forward may seem daunting, embracing openness to new relationships honors both our past bonds and future possibilities.

Each step toward healing - whether through support groups, volunteer work, or gradual exposure to new animal companions - builds emotional resilience. These experiences demonstrate that protecting ourselves from future pain often means missing opportunities for joy, growth, and meaningful connections.

The decision to welcome a new pet into our lives doesn't erase or diminish past relationships. Instead, it represents a conscious choice to expand our capacity for love and companionship. Our previous pets taught us invaluable lessons about unconditional love, trust, and the beauty of the human-animal bond. These lessons become the foundation for future relationships, enriching rather than replacing our memories.

Moving forward doesn't mean forgetting. It means carrying the wisdom, love, and experiences from our past relationships into new chapters of our lives. The vulnerability required to open our hearts again becomes an act of courage, honoring both our resilience and our capacity to heal.

By acknowledging and working through our fears about future loss, we discover that the rewards of companionship far outweigh the risks of heartbreak. Each new relationship offers unique opportunities for growth, joy, and healing - not as replacements for what was lost, but as additions to our ever-expanding circle of love.

CHAPTER 18

PREPARING YOUR HEART: BALANCING GRIEF AND JOY

Those final weeks with Max were agonizing. The lymphoma ravaged his golden body, the chemo sapping his spirit and zest for life. Despite our best efforts, we knew his time was drawing near. My wife and I struggled to stay strong for our kids, but the looming goodbye weighed heavily.

Each morning, I'd quietly let Max out, cherishing those small moments. His tail barely wagged, his steps slowing with fatigue. I stroked his muzzle, his brown eyes filled with a wisdom only the canine elderly possess. "Not long now, old friend," I'd whisper, my voice catching.

The night we lost him, a profound silence enveloped our home. The kids cried themselves to sleep, Max's empty bed a cruel reminder. In those darkest hours, I wondered if we'd ever be ready for another dog to bound through the door, to fill that gaping void with fresh love and unbridled puppy antics. For the first time, the thought brought me more sadness than solace.

Finding Joy While Honoring Grief

Grief and joy often feel like opposing forces, particularly when contemplating bringing a new pet into our lives. The weight of loss can make moments of happiness feel wrong or disloyal to our departed companion's memory. Yet these emotions aren't mutually exclusive - they exist in a delicate dance that reflects the complexity of the human heart.

Consider grief as waves on a shore. Some days, the tide rises high, flooding us with memories and longing. Other days, it recedes enough to reveal glimpses of joy peeking through like shells in the sand. Both states are natural, valid, and worthy of acknowledgment.

When joy emerges - perhaps while watching a playful puppy or feeling the purr of a shelter cat - it doesn't diminish the depth of love felt for our previous pet. That bond remains sacred and untouchable. Joy simply represents our heart's remarkable capacity to expand and heal.

This emotional duality manifests in various ways. You might laugh at a funny pet video, then feel a pang of sadness remembering similar moments with your own companion. Or you could experience excitement about potentially adopting, followed by guilt about "replacing" your lost friend. These swinging emotions reflect healthy processing rather than betrayal.

The presence of joy doesn't signal the end of grieving. Instead, it demonstrates the heart's ability to hold multiple truths simultaneously: the profound impact of loss alongside the potential for new connections. This capacity for emotional complexity speaks to the depth of human resilience and our innate need for companionship.

Allowing ourselves to experience moments of happiness honors our lost pet's legacy. After all, they brought immeasurable joy to our lives. By remaining open to future moments of delight, we carry forward their gift of teaching us how to love unconditionally.

Managing Conflicting Feelings

Managing the emotional complexity of pet loss while considering a new companion requires gentle self-reflection and practical coping strategies. When conflicting feelings arise, acknowledge them without judgment - they represent the depth of your capacity to love.

Journaling serves as a powerful tool for processing these mixed emotions. Set aside quiet time each day to explore your feelings on paper. Write freely about your departed pet, your fears about moving forward, and your hopes for future companionship. Consider prompts like "What excites me about potentially loving another pet?" or "What worries make me hesitate?" Let your thoughts flow without censoring or critiquing them.

Creating separate journal sections can help organize these complex emotions. Dedicate one section to memories of your lost pet, another to processing current feelings, and a third to exploring future possibilities. This structure allows you to honor your grief while making space for new hopes to emerge.

Mindfulness practices help ground us in the present moment when emotions feel overwhelming. Try this simple exercise: Sit quietly and focus on your breath. When thoughts about the past or future arise, acknowledge them without attachment. Gently return your attention to your breathing. This practice builds awareness of your emotional state without becoming consumed by it.

Another helpful technique involves body scanning. Starting at your toes and moving upward, notice where you hold tension related to grief or anxiety. As you identify these areas, consciously release the tension through deep breaths. This physical awareness can help process emotional stress more effectively.

Remember that experiencing joy about a potential new pet doesn't diminish your love for your departed companion. Consider creating a gratitude ritual that honors both experiences. Each morning, write down one cherished memory of your lost pet and one positive thought about future possibilities. This practice reinforces that your heart has room for both grief and hope.

When guilt surfaces about considering a new pet, try reframing these thoughts. Instead of viewing it as "replacing" your lost companion, recognize it as expanding your capacity for love. Your previous pet taught you how to be a compassionate caregiver - sharing that gift with another animal honors their legacy.

Honoring the Past While Embracing the Future

Opening your heart to a new pet doesn't mean closing the door on cherished memories. Creating a dedicated tribute space in your home allows you to maintain a tangible connection with your departed companion while building new bonds. Consider setting up a memory shelf or corner with carefully chosen photographs, favorite toys, or a personalized memorial item. This physical space serves as a bridge between past and present, helping integrate your experiences of love and loss.

The presence of a tribute area can actually deepen your relationship with a new pet. As you care for your new companion, pausing at this special spot creates moments of reflection and gratitude. These quiet interactions remind us that each pet brings unique gifts to our lives, enriching rather than replacing previous bonds.

Sharing stories about your previous pet with your new companion creates another meaningful connection. While your new pet may not understand the words, they respond to the emotion and warmth in your voice. This practice helps process grief while building intimacy with your new friend. Try incorporating these storytelling moments into daily routines - perhaps during quiet evening cuddles or morning walks.

Consider keeping a memory book that chronicles special moments with your previous pet. Add new entries about how their influence shapes your current pet parenting journey. For example, note how lessons learned from your previous pet help you better understand your new companion's needs. This ongoing narrative honors your past pet's legacy while celebrating fresh experiences.

Some pet parents find comfort in creating rituals that bridge past and present. This might involve lighting a candle at your tribute space during special moments with your new pet, or saying goodnight to both your memorial area and your new companion. These simple acts acknowledge the continuity of love across different relationships.

Remember that your capacity to love grows with experience. Each pet relationship builds upon previous ones, creating layers of understanding and compassion. By consciously maintaining connections to past pets while nurturing new bonds, you create a richer, more meaningful journey of pet companionship.

Reflection

The journey of pet companionship forms an endless circle of love, loss, and renewal. Each relationship builds upon the lessons and memories of those before, creating a tapestry of experiences that enrich our lives. By consciously maintaining connections to our past pets while opening our hearts to new companions, we honor both the timeless bonds we've forged and the fresh connections waiting to bloom.

Creating physical spaces and meaningful rituals helps bridge these transitions. Whether through a quiet memorial corner, shared stories, or simple daily acknowledgments, these practices ground us in gratitude for all our animal friends - past and present. These tangible reminders serve not as anchors to grief, but as foundations for building deeper, more nuanced relationships with new pets.

The path forward doesn't require choosing between honoring a departed pet and loving a new one. Instead, it invites us to expand our hearts, allowing space for both cherished memories and fresh beginnings. Each pet teaches us unique lessons about love, companionship, and resilience. These lessons accumulate, making us more compassionate and understanding caregivers with each new relationship.

By embracing this continuous cycle of pet companionship, we transform loss into legacy. Our departed pets live on through the wisdom they've shared, shaping how we bond with and care for future animal friends. Their influence ripples forward, touching each new relationship with added depth and meaning.

Remember that moving forward with a new pet while maintaining connections to the past isn't just possible - it's natural and healing. This balanced approach allows us to grow through our experiences while keeping precious memories alive, creating a richer, more fulfilling journey of pet parenthood.

CHAPTER 19

CELEBRATING NEW COMPANIONS: HONORING BOTH OLD AND NEW BONDS

The memories of Max are etched into every corner of my home - his favorite sunny spot for napping, the squeaky toy he loved to chase, even the slight indentations his paws left on the couch cushions. At first, these reminders felt like salt in an open wound, intensifying the ache of his absence. But slowly, I began seeing them as connections to the profound love we shared rather than constant reminders of loss.

I created a small memorial shelf with his collar, some photos, and a clay paw print to honor the ways he enriched my life. On difficult days, I'd light a candle beside it, basking in the warm glow as I reminisced about Max's gentle spirit. With each passing season, considering adopting another pup became less daunting. Though Max can never be replaced, I knew opening my heart to a new companion would be the greatest tribute I could give his memory.

Embracing New Beginnings

Opening your heart to a new pet brings unexpected moments of delight and discovery. Each animal arrives with their own distinct personality - perhaps a cat who insists on sleeping in the bathroom sink, or a dog who spins in circles before settling into their bed. These quirks and characteristics emerge gradually, like petals unfurling in the morning sun.

The process of getting to know a new companion creates natural opportunities for joy. You might notice how they tilt their head when curious, or the specific way they request attention. These small discoveries build into a unique language between you and your pet, forming the foundation of your special bond.

New routines develop organically as you learn each other's rhythms. Morning walks might take unexpected detours as your dog shows interest in different routes. Feeding times transform into bonding moments when you notice their enthusiasm for certain treats or toys. Even quiet evenings take on fresh meaning as you observe their preferred spots for relaxation.

These daily interactions create space for new traditions. Maybe your pet gravitates toward certain games, leading to regular play sessions that become cherished parts of your day. Or perhaps they show excitement for specific activities, like joining you in the garden or cuddling during morning coffee.

The joy multiplies as you witness their confidence grow within your home. A formerly shy rescue cat might start claiming favorite windowsills, while a tentative puppy develops into an enthusiastic playmate. Each small step forward reinforces the developing trust between you.

Documenting these early moments helps preserve the magic of your budding relationship. Taking photos of first experiences, noting funny behaviors, or recording special milestones creates a treasury of memories from the start. These captured moments become the building blocks of your shared story.

Remember that each new pet brings their own gifts to your life. By staying present and receptive to these unique offerings, you allow natural joy to flourish in this fresh chapter of pet companionship.

Honoring Past and Present Bonds

Creating space for both past and present pets allows love to expand rather than replace. Consider setting up a dedicated memorial area that celebrates your previous pet while welcoming your new companion. A thoughtfully arranged shelf or corner might display your former pet's favorite toy alongside current photos, bridging the connection between then and now.

Welcome ceremonies help mark the beginning of your new journey while acknowledging what came before. Light a candle in memory of your previous pet, then introduce your new family member to special spots around your home. Share stories about your past pet as you create fresh memories, letting their legacy inspire new traditions.

Photo displays can beautifully capture the continuity of love across different relationships. Arrange images that show meaningful moments with both pets - perhaps your previous dog at their favorite park alongside new snapshots of your current companion exploring the same space. These visual reminders reinforce that your heart has room for multiple bonds.

Include elements of your previous pet's life in ways that feel natural with your new companion. Their old walking route might become a special adventure for your current pet, with stops to remember shared moments. Or their favorite treat spot could transform into a place where both pets' memories intertwine.

Consider creating rituals that honor both relationships. Monthly remembrance days might include looking through old photos before taking your new pet on an outing. Special occasions like adoption anniversaries become opportunities to celebrate all the joy your pets have brought into your life.

Remember that embracing a new pet doesn't diminish your love for those who came before. Each relationship stands unique, contributing its own chapters to your story of pet companionship. By consciously making space for both past and present bonds, you create a rich tapestry of memories and experiences that enhance each other.

Reflection

The journey of honoring both past and present pet bonds requires gentle patience and intentional practice. Through thoughtful rituals and meaningful ceremonies, we create sacred spaces where grief and joy can coexist peacefully. These practices help us navigate the complex emotions that arise when opening our hearts to new companionship while cherishing precious memories.

By acknowledging that each pet relationship enriches our capacity for love rather than diminishing previous bonds, we free ourselves from unnecessary guilt or hesitation. The rituals we create serve as bridges between past and present, allowing us to move forward while keeping cherished memories close.

Whether through simple daily practices like lighting candles and writing letters, or larger seasonal celebrations that honor multiple pets, these meaningful activities anchor us in both remembrance and presence. They remind us that love's capacity grows endlessly, making room for new bonds while treasuring those who came before.

The path of pet companionship teaches us that our hearts expand to hold both loss and love, memory and hope, past and present. By consciously creating spaces and practices that honor all our animal friends, we embrace the full spectrum of what it means to love deeply and continue loving, even after loss.

This integration of past and present bonds ultimately enriches our experience as pet guardians, allowing each relationship to add its unique thread to the tapestry of our lives. Through these intentional practices, we learn that remembrance and new beginnings need not compete, but rather complement and strengthen each other in beautiful ways.

CHAPTER 20

A JOURNEY OF LOVE AND HEALING: EMBRACING HOPE, REFLECTION, AND RESILIENCE AFTER PET LOSS

The Path of Healing

From the moment we invited our beloved pets into our lives, we embarked on a profound journey of companionship and love. This unbreakable bond became woven into the fabric of our daily existence, enriching our lives with loyalty, laughter, and an unparalleled connection. However, the harsh reality is that our cherished animal friends cannot remain by our sides forever. The heart-wrenching experience of pet loss thrusts us into an unfamiliar emotional landscape flooded with grief.

This book has served as your steadfast companion through the turbulent waters of bereavement. We began by acknowledging the legitimacy of your sorrow, countering societal misconceptions that often diminish the significance of pet loss. Through candid explorations of complex emotions like guilt, anger, and depression, you gained validation for your innermost feelings during this trying time.

As we delved deeper, you discovered a toolbox of coping strategies to navigate the fluctuating tides of grief. From the healing powers of mindfulness and journaling to the solace found in rituals and personal keepsakes, this book equipped you with tangible methods to express your love and find moments of peace. We also addressed the profound impact on children, providing age-appropriate guidance to support their journeys.

Our path then turned toward the light of healing, as we examined avenues for memorialization and paying tribute to your pet's enduring legacy. Throughout this transformative expedition, we confronted the harsh realities and intense emotions associated with profound loss. Yet, even in the depths of sorrow, we uncovered the resilience of the human spirit and its ability to embrace hope once more.

Key Takeaways

As we approach the culmination of our journey together, let us reflect on the invaluable lessons and insights gained throughout the pages of this book. We have learned that the grief experienced after losing a beloved pet is a natural and valid emotional response, one that deserves recognition and compassion.

The path to healing is rarely linear, and we must embrace the ebb and flow of our emotions, allowing ourselves to experience the full spectrum of feelings without judgment or self-imposed timelines. Through this process, we have discovered the power of self-compassion, learning to forgive ourselves for the decisions made and the regrets harbored.

We have explored practical coping mechanisms, such as journaling, mindfulness practices, and the creation of personal rituals and keepsakes, which have provided solace and a means of expression during our most vulnerable moments. These tools have not only aided in processing our grief but have also fostered a deeper connection with the cherished memories of our departed companions.

Moreover, we have acknowledged the profound impact of pet loss on children and the importance of open communication, age-appropriate explanations, and creative outlets to support their emotional well-being. By nurturing their understanding and providing a safe space for expression, we can guide them through this challenging transition.

Throughout our journey, we have also confronted societal misconceptions and insensitive remarks, learning to respond with grace and empathy while advocating for greater awareness and understanding of the human-animal bond. By sharing our stories and experiences, we can contribute to a cultural shift that recognizes the significance of pet loss and the need for support during this difficult time.

As we look ahead, we carry with us the wisdom gained from navigating the depths of grief, a resilience forged by embracing vulnerability and the courage to open our hearts once more to the possibility of new connections and relationships.

Hope and Healing

It is essential to carry within our hearts an unwavering belief in the possibility of hope and healing. While the pain of losing a cherished companion can feel insurmountable, we must remember that this grief is a testament to the profound love and companionship we shared with our beloved pets.

The path to healing is not a linear one, nor is it the same for everyone. It is a deeply personal odyssey, woven with moments of joy, sorrow, and self-discovery. However, by embracing the insights and tools provided within these pages, you possess the power to navigate this challenging terrain with grace and resilience.

Throughout our exploration, we have learned the importance of acknowledging and validating our emotions, for it is only through this acceptance that we can begin to heal. We have discovered the transformative power of self-compassion, forgiving ourselves for the decisions made and the regrets harbored, and embracing the journey with kindness and understanding.

The coping mechanisms we have explored – from journaling and mindfulness practices to the creation of personal rituals and keepsakes – have provided solace and a means of expression during our most vulnerable moments. These tools have not only aided in processing our grief but have also fostered a deeper connection with the cherished memories of our departed companions, ensuring their enduring presence in our lives.

As we look ahead, it is crucial to hold onto the belief that healing is not only possible but an inevitable destination for those who embrace the journey with courage and compassion. While the path may be winding and the terrain challenging at times, each step taken is a testament to the resilience of the human spirit and the enduring power of love.

Remember, you are not alone in this journey. Countless others have walked this path before you, and their stories serve as beacons of hope, illuminating the way forward. Embrace the wisdom and support offered by this community, for it is through shared experiences that we can find strength and solace.

The Power of Ongoing Reflection

As you continue on your path towards healing, it is essential to recognize the power of ongoing reflection. The journey of pet loss grief is not one with a definitive endpoint but rather an evolving process that requires continued introspection and self-discovery.

The tools and techniques provided throughout this book, such as journaling prompts and mindfulness exercises, are not meant to be used only once and then discarded. Instead, they are designed to be revisited and incorporated into your daily life as ongoing resources for recovery and personal growth.

Journaling, in particular, can serve as a powerful outlet for exploring your emotions and experiences. By dedicating time each day to write about your thoughts, feelings, and memories, you create a safe space for self-expression and reflection. This practice allows you to process your grief at your own pace, uncovering insights and revelations that may have been previously hidden beneath the surface of your consciousness.

Similarly, mindfulness exercises offer a means of cultivating present-moment awareness and emotional regulation. By incorporating techniques such as deep breathing, body scans, and guided imagery into your daily routine, you can develop a greater sense of grounding and stability amidst the turbulence of grief.

As you engage in these practices consistently, you may find that your perspective begins to shift. Memories that once evoked painful emotions may gradually transform into sources of comfort and gratitude. The lessons learned from your journey with your beloved pet may reveal themselves in new and profound ways, enriching your understanding of love, loss, and resilience.

It is important to approach this ongoing reflection with patience and self-compassion. There will be days when the practice feels challenging or even overwhelming. In these moments, remember to be kind to yourself, acknowledging that healing is not a linear process and that setbacks are a natural part of the journey.

By committing to ongoing reflection, you honor the memory of your cherished companion and the transformative impact they had on your life. You create space for growth, healing, and the cultivation of newfound wisdom and strength.

AFTERWORD

The blank pages of my journal became a sanctuary in the months after Max's passing. Each entry captured fragments of our life together - the way he'd rest his chin on my knee during thunderstorms, his excited dance when I grabbed the leash, the gentle thump of his tail against the hardwood floor. Writing helped make sense of the profound emptiness his absence left behind.

Those pages now serve as a precious archive of our journey through grief. When I flip through them today, I find not just sorrow, but celebration of the pure joy Max brought to our family for eight wonderful years. His battle with lymphoma may have been brief, but his impact on our lives remains eternal.

Creating this book allowed me to transform my personal healing process into what I hope becomes a source of comfort for others walking this difficult path. Each chapter emerged from my own experience, informed by those raw journal entries that helped me process my pain one word at a time.

The house felt different after Max - quieter, emptier. For months, I'd catch myself listening for the click of his nails on the floor or reaching down to scratch behind ears that weren't there. We talked about getting another dog, but the timing never felt right. The grief still felt too raw, too present.

Then one spring morning, almost a year after losing Max, I woke up ready. Not to replace him - no dog could ever do that - but to open our hearts to love again. We found ourselves scrolling online for breeders, studying fuzzy photos of wagging tails and hopeful eyes.

That's how we met Bailey. He bounded into the breeder's living room, all gangly legs and uncoordinated puppy energy. While Max had been dignified and gentle, Bailey was pure chaos wrapped in golden fur. He crashed into chairs, attempted to eat my shoelaces, and then flopped onto his back for belly rubs.

"He's nothing like Max," my wife whispered, watching Bailey zoom around the room.

"Maybe that's exactly what we need," I replied.

Taking Bailey home felt both familiar and entirely new. The old routines returned - morning walks, feeding times, training sessions - but Bailey put his own spin on everything. Where Max had been content to watch squirrels from afar, Bailey wanted to chase every single one. Where Max had gracefully navigated furniture, Bailey bounced off walls and skidded across floors.

Some days, watching Bailey discover the world reminded me of Max's puppy days. Other times, the differences between them brought unexpected comfort. Bailey wasn't trying to fill Max's paw prints - he was creating his own path, teaching us new ways to laugh and love.

Hanging Max's collar next to Bailey's on our key hook felt right. Our hearts had grown to hold both - the cherished memories of one beloved dog and the daily adventures of another. Bailey helped us remember that love wasn't finite, that opening our hearts again didn't diminish what we'd shared with Max.

This book represents not just my journey of loss and renewal, but a testament to the profound bonds we forge with our animal companions. Through sharing these words, I've discovered that grief, when expressed openly, can transform into deeper appreciation for the gifts our pets leave behind - the lessons of unconditional love, living in the moment, and finding joy in life's simple pleasures.

To those reading these pages while navigating their own loss - may you find solace in knowing your pain is valid, your memories are precious, and your heart will heal in its own time. The journey through grief is deeply personal, but you don't have to walk it alone.

MAKE A DIFFERENCE WITH YOUR REVIEW

Share Your Journey to Help Others Heal

"Until one has loved an animal, a part of one's soul remains unawakened." – Anatole France

The bond we share with our pets is unlike any other. They become our companions, our comfort, and our family. When we lose them, the grief can feel overwhelming—but together, we can find healing.

Would you help someone like you—someone navigating the heartache of losing a beloved pet—by sharing your thoughts on *Goodbye, Friend: A Journey Through Pet Loss and Grieving*?

My mission is to bring comfort, hope, and understanding to everyone experiencing the loss of a cherished animal companion. Your review can help others decide if this book might guide them through their own journey of healing.

Most people choose books based on reviews. When you take a moment to share your experience, you're offering support to someone who may be feeling lost and alone. Your review could help...

- ...one more person find the words to explain their grief.

- ...one more pet parent feel less isolated in their sadness.

- ...one more reader discover a path toward peace and healing.

It costs nothing and takes less than a minute, but your words could make all the difference.

To leave your review, simply scan the QR code or visit the link below:

If you believe in the power of kindness and connection, you're my kind of person. Thank you from the bottom of my heart for sharing your thoughts and helping others find their way.

Warmly,
Owen Whitmore